Lafcadio Hearn

Stray Leaves from Strange Literature

Stories Reconstructed from the Anvari-Soheïli, Baitál, Pachísí....

Lafcadio Hearn

Stray Leaves from Strange Literature
Stories Reconstructed from the Anvari-Soheïli, Baitál, Pachísi....

ISBN/EAN: 9783337202927

Printed in Europe, USA, Canada, Australia, Japan

Cover: Foto ©Thomas Meinert / pixelio.de

More available books at **www.hansebooks.com**

STRAY LEAVES

FROM

STRANGE LITERATURE

STRAY LEAVES FROM STRANGE LITERATURE

Stories

RECONSTRUCTED FROM THE ANVARI-SOHEÏLI,
BAITÁL PACHÍSÍ, MAHABHARATA, PANTCHA-
TANTRA, GULISTAN, TALMUD, KALEWALA, ETC.

BY LAFCADIO HEARN

BOSTON AND NEW YORK
HOUGHTON MIFFLIN COMPANY
The Riverside Press Cambridge

𝕿𝖔 𝖒𝖞 𝕱𝖗𝖎𝖊𝖓𝖉,

PAGE M. BAKER,

EDITOR OF THE

NEW ORLEANS TIMES-DEMOCRAT.

EXPLANATORY.

WHILE engaged upon this little mosaic work of legend and fable, I felt much like one of those merchants told of in Sindbad's Second Voyage, who were obliged to content themselves with gathering the small jewels adhering to certain meat which eagles brought up from the Valley of Diamonds. I have had to depend altogether upon the labor of translators for my acquisitions; and these seemed too small to deserve separate literary setting. By cutting my little gems according to one pattern, I have doubtless reduced the beauty of some; yet it seemed to me their colors were so weird, their luminosity so elfish, that their intrinsic value could not be wholly destroyed even by so clumsy an artificer as I.

In short, these fables, legends, parables, etc., are simply reconstructions of what impressed me

as most fantastically beautiful in the most exotic
literature which I was able to obtain. With few
exceptions, the plans of the original narratives
have been preserved. Sometimes I have added
a little, sometimes curtailed ; but the augmenta-
tions were generally made with material drawn
from the same source as the legend, while the
abbreviations were effected either with a view
to avoid repetition, or through the necessity of
suppressing incidents unsuited to the general
reading. I must call special attention to certain romantic liberties or poetic licenses which
I have taken.

In the Polynesian story ("The Fountain Maid-
en") I have considerably enlarged upon the
legend, which I found in Gill's "Myths and
Songs of the South Pacific," — a curious but
inartistic book, in which much admirable material has been very dryly handled. In another
portion of Mr. Gill's book I found the text and
translation of the weird "Thieves' Song ;" and
conceived the idea of utilizing it in the story,
with some fanciful changes. The Arabic "Legend of Love" is still more apocryphal, as it
consists of fragmentary Arabian stories, borrowed
from De Stendahl's "L'Amour," and welded into
one narrative.

In the Rabbinical legends I have often united several incidents related about one personage in various of the Talmudic treatises ; but this system is sufficiently specified by references to the "Gemara" in the text. By consulting the indices attached to Hershon's Miscellany, and Schwab's translations of the Jerusalem Talmud, it was easy to collect a number of singular traditions attaching to one distinguished Rabbi, and to unite these into a narrative. Finally, I must confess that the story of "Natalika" was not drawn directly from Ferista, or Fihristah, but from Jacolliot, a clever writer, but untrustworthy Orientalist, whose books have little serious value. Whether true or false, however, the legend of the statue seemed to me too pretty to overlook.

In one case only have I made a veritable translation from the French. Léouzon Le Duc's literal version of the "Kalewala" seemed to me the most charming specimen of poetical prose I had met with among translations. I selected three incidents, and translated them almost word for word.

Nearly all of the Italic texts, although fancifully arranged, have been drawn from the literatures of those peoples whose legends they introduce. Many phrases were obtained from

that inexhaustible treasury of Indian wisdom, the
"Pantchatantra;" others from various Buddhist
works. The introductory text of the piece, enti-
tled "The King's Justice," was borrowed from
the Persian "Mantic Uttaïr," of Farid Uddin
Attar; and the text at the commencement of the
Buddhist Parable (which was refashioned after
a narrative in Stanislas Julien's "Avadanas")
was taken from the "Dhammapada." The briefer
stories, I think, have generally suffered less at
my hands than the lengthier ones. That wonderful Egyptian romance about the Book of
Thoth is far more striking in Maspéro's French
translations from the original papyrus; but the
Egyptian phrases are often characterized by a
nakedness rather more startling than that of the
dancing girls in the mural paintings. . . .

Upon another page will be found a little
bibliography of nearly all the sources whence I
have drawn my material. Some volumes are
mentioned only because they gave me one or
two phrases. Thus, I borrowed expressions or
ideas from "Amarou,". from Fauche's translation
of the "Ritou Sanhara," and especially from the
wealth of notes to Chézy's superb translation of
"Sacountala."

This little collection has no claim upon the

consideration of scholars. It is simply an attempt to share with the public some of those novel delights I experienced while trying to familiarize myself with some very strange and beautiful literatures.

During its preparation two notable works have appeared with a partly similar purpose: Helen Zimmern's "Epic of Kings," and Edwin Arnold's "Rosary of Islam." In the former we have a charming popular version of Firdusi, and upon the latter are exquisitely strung some of the fairest pearls of the "Mesnewi." I hope my far less artistic contribution to the popularization of unfamiliar literature may stimulate others to produce something worthier than I can hope to do. My gems were few and small: the monstrous and splendid await the coming of Sindbad, or some mighty lapidary by whom they may be wrought into jewel bouquets exquisite as those bunches of topaz blossoms and ruby buds laid upon the tomb of Nourmahal.

New Orleans, 1884.

BIBLIOGRAPHY.

———◆———

(There are very fine English translations of the works marked with an asterisk.)

ALLEGORIES, RÉCITS, CONTES, etc., traduits de l'Arabe, du Persan, de l'Hindustani, et du Turc. Par M. Garcin de Tassy. Paris, 1876. (Includes "Bakawali.")

AMAROU. *Anthologie Erotique.* Texte sanscrit, traduction, notes, etc., par A. L. Apudy (Chézy). Paris, 1831.

AVADANAS (LES). *Contes et Apologues Indiens.* Traduits par M. Stanislas Julien. Paris, 1859.

BUDDHA (ROMANTIC LEGEND OF). Translated by Rev. Samuel Beal. London, 1875.

CONTES ÉGYPTIENS. Par G. Maspéro. Paris, 1882.

DHAMMAPADA (THE). Translated from the Chinese by Rev. Samuel Beal, B.A. Boston, 1878.

*GITA-GOVINDA (LE), ET LE RITOU-SANHARA. Traduits par Hippolyte Fauche. Paris, 1850.

*GULISTAN (LE), DE SADI. Traduit littéralement, par N. Semelet. Paris, 1834.

HINDOO PANTHEON (THE). By Major Edward Moor. London, 1861.

*Hitopadésa (L'). Traduit par E. Lancereau. Paris, 1882.

Jacolliot. *Voyage aux Ruines de Golconde.* Paris, 1878.

Jataka-Tales. Translated by T. W. Rhuys Davids. Vol. I. Boston, 1881.

Kalewala. Traduction de Léouzon Le Duc. Paris, 1845.

Mahabharata (Onze Épisodes du). Traduit par Foucaux. Paris, 1862.

*Mantic Uttaïr. Traduit du Persan par M. Garcin de Tassy. Paris, 1863.

Mythologie des Esquimaux. Par l'Abbé Morillot. Paris, 1874.

Myths and Songs of the South Pacific. By Rev. W. W. Gill. London, 1877.

*Pantchatantra ; ou, Les Cinq Livres. Traduit par E. Lancereau. Paris, 1871.

Stendahl (De). *L'Amour.*

*Sacountala. Texte sanscrit, notes et traduction par Chézy. Paris. 1830.

Talmud. *Le Talmud de Jerusalem.* Traduit par Moïse Schwab. Vols. I.–VI. Paris, 1878–83.

Talmudic Miscellany (A). By Rev. L. P. Hershon. Boston, 1882.

Vetálapanchavinsatí (Hindi Version of the). *Baitál Pachísí ; or, The Twenty-five Tales of a Demon.* Translated by W. B. Barker. London, 1855.

CONTENTS.

STRAY LEAVES.

THE BOOK OF THOTH.

*An Egyptian tale of weirdness, as told in a demotic papy-
rus found in the necropolis of Deir-el-Medineh among the
ruins of hundred-gated Thebes. . . . Written in the thirty-
fifth year of the reign of some forgotten Ptolomœus, and in the
month of Tybi completed by a scribe famous among magicians. . . . Dedicated, doubtless, to Thoth, Lord of all Scribes,
Grand Master of all Sorcerers; whose grace had been rever-
ently invoked upon whomsoever might speak well concerning
the same papyrus. . . .*

. . . THOTH, the divine, lord of scribes, most
excellent of workers, prince of wizards, once, it
is said, wrote with his own hand a book sur-
passing all other books, and containing two magical formulas only. Whosoever could recite the
first of these formulas would become forthwith
second only to the gods, — for by its simple utterance the mountains and the valleys, the ocean

and the clouds, the heights of heaven and the deeps of hell, would be made subject unto his will; while the birds of air, the reptiles of darkness, and the fishes of the waters, would be thereby compelled to appear, and to make manifest the thoughts secreted within their hearts. But whosoever could recite the second formula might never know death, — for even though buried within the entrails of the earth, he would still behold heaven through the darkness and hear the voices of earth athwart the silence; even in the necropolis he would still see the rising and setting of the sun, and the Cycle of the Gods, and the waxing and waning of the moon, and the eternal lights of the firmament.

And the god Thoth deposited his book within a casket of gold, and the casket of gold within a casket of silver, and the casket of silver within a casket of ivory and ebony, and the casket of ivory and ebony within a casket of palm-wood, and the casket of palm-wood within a casket of bronze, and the casket of bronze within a casket of iron. And he buried the same in the bed of the great river of Egypt where it flows through the Nome of Coptos; and immortal river monsters coiled about the casket to guard it from all magicians.

⁎

Now, of all magicians, Noferkephtah, the son of King Minibphtah (to whom be life, health, and strength forevermore!), first by cunning discovered the place where the wondrous book was hidden, and found courage to possess himself thereof. (For after he had well paid the wisest of the ancient priests to direct his way, Noferkephtah obtained from his father Pharaoh a royal cangia, well supplied and stoutly manned, wherein he journeyed to Coptos in search of the hidden treasure. Coming to Coptos after many days, he created him a magical boat and a magical crew by reciting mystic words; and he and the shadowy crew with him toiled to find the casket; and by the building of dams they were enabled to find it. Then Noferkephtah prevailed also against the immortal serpent by dint of sorcery; and he obtained the book, and read the mystic formulas) and made himself second only to the gods.

But the divinities, being wroth with him, caused his sister and wife Ahouri to fall into the Nile, and his son also. Noferkephtah indeed compelled the river to restore them; but although

the power of the book maintained their life after
a strange fashion, they lived not as before, so
that he had to bury them in the necropolis at
Coptos. Seeing these things and fearing to return
to the king alone, he tied the book above his
heart, and also allowed himself to drown. The
power of the book, indeed, maintained his life
after a strange fashion; but he lived not as before, so that they took him back to Thebes as one
who had passed over to Amenthi, and there laid
him with his fathers, and the book also.]

Yet, by the power of the book, he lived within
the darkness of the tomb, and beheld the sun
rising, and the Cycle of the Gods, and the phases
of the moon, and the stars of the night. By the
power of the book, also, he summoned to him
the shadow of his sister Ahouri, buried at Coptos, — whom he had made his wife according to
the custom of the Egyptians; and there was light
within their dwelling-place. Thus Noferkephtah
knew ghostly happiness in the company of the
Ka, or shadow, of his wife Ahouri, and the *Ka*
of his son Mikhonsou.

_{*}

Now, four generations had passed since the time
of King Minibphtah; and the Pharaoh of Egypt
was Ousirmari. Ousirmari had two sons who

were learned among the Egyptians, — Satni was
the name of the elder; Anhathoreroou that of the
younger.   There was not in all Egypt so wise a
scribe as Satni. He knew how to read the sacred
writings, and the inscriptions upon the amulets,
and the sentences within the tombs, and the words
graven upon the stelæ, and the books of that
sacerdotal library called the "Double House of
Life."   Also he knew the composition of all formulas of sorcery and of all sentences which spirits obey, so that there was no enchanter like him
in all Egypt.   And Satni heard of Noferkephtah and the book of Thoth from a certain aged
priest, and resolved that he would obtain it.   But
the aged priest warned him, saying, "Beware
thou dost not wrest the book from Noferkephtah,
else thou wilt be enchanted by him, and compelled
to bear it back to him within the tomb, and do
great penance."

Nevertheless Satni sought and obtained permission of the king to descend into the necropolis of Thebes, and to take away, if he might, the
book from thence.   So he went thither with his
brother.

***

Three days and three nights the brothers sought
for the tomb of Noferkephtah in the immeasurable

city of the dead; and after they had threaded
many miles of black corridors, and descended
into many hundred burial pits, and were weary
with the deciphering of innumerable inscriptions
by quivering light of lamps, they found his resting-place at last. Now, when they entered the
tomb their eyes were dazzled; for Noferkephtah
was lying there with his wife Ahouri beside him;
and the book of Thoth, placed between them,
shed such a light around, that it seemed like the
brightness of the sun. And when Satni entered,
the Shadow of Ahouri rose against the light; and
she asked him, " Who art thou?"

Then Satni answered: "I am Satni, son of
King Ousirmari; and I come for the book of
Thoth which is between thee and Noferkephtah;
and if thou wilt not give it me, I shall wrest it
away by force."

But the Shadow of the woman replied to him:
" Nay, be not unreasoning in thy words! Do
not ask for this book. For we, in obtaining it,
were deprived of the pleasure of living upon earth
for the term naturally allotted us; neither is this
enchanted life within the tomb like unto the life
of Egypt. Nowise can the book serve thee; therefore listen rather to the recital of all those sorrows
which befell us by reason of this book. . . ."

But after hearing the story of Ahouri, the heart of Satni remained as bronze; and he only repeated : —

"If thou wilt not give me the book which is between thee and Noferkephtah, I shall wrest it away by force."

Then Noferkephtah rose up within the tomb, and laughed, saying : " O Satni, if thou art indeed a true scribe, win this book from me by thy skill! If thou art not afraid, play against me a game for the possession of this book, — a game of *fifty-two!*" Now there was a chess-board within the tomb.

Then Satni played a game of chess with Noferkephtah, while the *Kas*, the Shadows, the Doubles of Ahouri, and the large-eyed boy looked on. But the eyes with which they gazed upon him, and the eyes of Noferkephtah also, strangely disturbed him, so that Satni's brain whirled, and the web of his thought became entangled, and he lost! Noferkephtah laughed, and uttered a magical word, and placed the chess-board upon Satni's head; and Satni sank to his knees into the floor of the tomb.

Again they played, and the result was the same. Then Noferkephtah uttered another magical word, and again placed the chess-board upon Satni's

head; and Satni sank to his hips into the floor
of the tomb.

Once more they played, and the result was the
same.   Then Noferkephtah uttered a third magical word, and laid the chess-board on Satni's
head, and Satni sank up to his ears into the floor
of the tomb!

Then Satni shrieked to his brother to bring
him certain talismans quickly; and the brother
fetched the talismans, and placed them upon
Satni's head, and by magical amulets saved him
from the power of Noferkephtah.   But having
done this, Anhathorerôou fell dead within the
tomb.

And Satni put forth his hand and took the book
from Noferkephtah, and went out of the tomb
into the corridors; while the book lighted the
way for him, so that a great brightness travelled
before him, and deep blackness went after him.
Into the darkness Ahouri followed him, lament-
ing, and crying out: " Woe! woe upon us!   The
light that gave life is taken from us; the hideous
Nothingness will come upon us!   Now, indeed,
will annihilation enter into the tomb!"   But Noferkephtah called Ahouri to him, and bade her
cease to weep, saying to her: " Grieve not after
the book; for I shall make him bring it back to

me, with a fork and stick in his hand and a lighted
brazier upon his head."

* *

But when the king Ousirmari heard of all that
had taken place, he became very much alarmed
for his son, and said to him : "Behold ! thy folly
has already caused the death of thy brother Anhathoreroou ; take heed, therefore, lest it bring
about thine own destruction likewise. Noferkephtah dead is even a mightier magician than
thou. Take back the book forthwith, lest he
destroy thee."

And Satni replied : "Lo ! never have I owned
a sensual wish, nor done evil to *living* creature ;
how, then, can the dead prevail against me? It
is only the foolish scribe — the scribe who hath
not learned the mastery of passions — that may
be overcome by enchantment."

And he kept the book.

* *

Now it came to pass that a few days after,
while Satni stood upon the parvise of the temple of Pthah, he beheld a woman so beautiful
that from the moment his eyes fell upon her he
ceased to act like one living, and all the world
grew like a dream about him. And while the
young woman was praying in the temple, Satni

heard that her name was Thoutboui, daughter of a prophet. Whereupon he sent a messenger to her, saying: "Thus declares my master: I, the Prince Satni, son of King Ousirmari, do so love thee that I feel as one about to die. . . . If thou wilt love me as I desire, thou shalt have kingliest gifts; otherwise, know that I have the power to bury thee alive among the dead, so that none may ever see thee again."

And Thoutboui on hearing these words appeared not at all astonished, nor angered, nor terrified; but her great black eyes laughed, and she answered, saying: "Tell thy master, Prince Satni, son of King Ousirmari, to visit me within my house at Bubastes, whither I am even now going.". . . Thereupon she went away with her retinue of maidens.

* * *

So Satni hastened forthwith to Bubastes by the river, and to the house of Thoutboui, the prophet's daughter. In all the place there was no house like unto her house; it was lofty and long, and surrounded by a garden all encircled with a white wall. And Satni followed Thoutboui's serving-maid into the house, and by a coiling stairway to an upper chamber wherein were broad beds of ebony and ivory, and rich furniture curiously carved, and tripods with burning perfumes, and tables of cedar with cups of gold. And the walls were coated with lapis-lazuli inlaid with emerald, making a strange and pleasant light. . . . Thoutboui appeared upon the threshold, robed in textures of white, transparent as the dresses of those dancing women limned upon the walls of the Pharaohs' palace ; and as she stood against the light, Satni, beholding the litheness of her limbs, the flexibility of her body, felt his heart cease to beat within him, so that he could not speak. But she served him with wine, and took from his hands the gifts which he had brought,— and she suffered him to kiss her.

Then said Thoutboui : " Not lightly is my love to be bought with gifts. Yet will I test thee, since thou dost so desire. If thou wilt be loved by me, therefore, make over to me by deed all thou hast, — thy gold and thy silver, thy lands and houses, thy goods and all that belongs to thee. So that the house wherein I dwell may become thy house ! "

And Satni, looking into the long black jewels of her eyes, forgot the worth of all that he possessed ; and a scribe was summoned, and the scribe drew up the deed giving to Thoutboui all the goods of Satni.

Then said Thoutboui: "Still will I test thee, since thou dost so desire. If thou wilt have my love, make over to me thy children, also, as my slaves, lest they should seek dispute with my children concerning that which was thine. So that the house in which I dwell may become thy house!"

And Satni, gazing upon the witchery of her bosom, curved like ivory carving, rounded like the eggs of the ostrich, forgot his loving children; and the deed was written. . . . Even at that moment a messenger came, saying: "O Satni, thy children are below, and await thee." And he said: "Bid them ascend hither."

Then said Thoutboui: "Still will I test thee, since thou dost so desire. If thou wilt have my love, let thy children be put to death, lest at some future time they seek to claim that which thou hast given. So that the house in which I dwell may be thy house!"

And Satni, enchanted with the enchantment of her pliant stature, of her palmy grace, of her ivorine beauty, forgot even his fatherhood, and answered: "Be it so; were I ruler of heaven, even heaven would I give thee for a kiss."

Then Thoutboui had the children of Satni slain before his eyes; yet he sought not to save them!

She bade her servant cast their bodies from the windows to the cats and to the dogs below; yet Satni lifted not his hand to prevent it! And while he drank wine with Thoutboui, he could hear the growling of the animals that were eating the flesh of his children. But he only moaned to her: "Give me thy love! I am as one in hell for thy sake!" And she arose, and, entering another chamber, turned and held out her wonderful arms to him, and drew him to her with the sorcery of her unutterable eyes. . . .

But as Satni sought to clasp her and to kiss her, lo! her ruddy mouth opened and extended and broadened and deepened, — yawning wider, darker, quickly, vastly, — a blackness as of necropoles, a vastness as of Amenthi! And Satni beheld only a gulf before him, deepening and shadowing like night; and from out the gulf a burst of tempest roared up, and bore him with it, and whirled him abroad as a leaf. And his senses left him. . . .

***

. . . When he came again to himself, he was lying naked at the entrance of the subterranean sepulchres; and a great horror and despair came upon him, so that he purposed ending his life. But the servants of the king found him, and bore him safely to his father. And Ousirmari heard the ghostly tale.

Then said Ousirmari: "O Satni, Noferkephtah dead is a mightier magician than even thou living. Know, my son, first of all that thy children are alive and well in my own care; know, also, that the woman by whose beauty thou wert bewitched, and for whom thou hast in thought committed all heinous crimes, was a phantom wrought by Noferkephtah's magic. Thus, by exciting thee to passion, did he bring thy magical power to nought. And now, my dear son, haste with the book to Noferkephtah, lest thou perish utterly, with all thy kindred."

So Satni took the book of Thoth, and, carrying a fork and stick in his hands and a lighted brazier upon his head, carried it to the Theban necropolis and into the tomb of Noferkephtah. And Ahouri clapped her hands, and smiled to see the light again return. And Noferkephtah laughed, saying: "Did I not tell thee beforehand?" "Aye!" said Ahouri, "thou wert enchanted, O Satni!" But Satni, prostrating himself before Noferkephtah, asked how he might make atonement.

"O Satni," answered Noferkephtah, "my wife and my son are indeed buried at Coptos; these whom thou seest here are their Doubles only, — their Shadows, their *Kas*, — maintained with me by enchantment. Seek out their resting-place at Coptos, therefore, and bury their bodies with me, that we may all be thus reunited, and that thou mayst do penance." . . .

So Satni went to Coptos, and there found an ancient priest, who told him the place of Ahouri's sepulture, saying : " The father of the father of my father told it to my father's father, who told it to my father." . . . Then Satni found the bodies, and restored to Noferkephtah his wife and his son ; and thus did penance. After which the tomb of Noferkephtah was sealed up forever by Pharaoh's order ; and no man knoweth more the place of Noferkephtah's sepulture.

THE FOUNTAIN MAIDEN.

A legend of that pacific land where garments are worn by none save the dead; where the beauty of youth is as the beauty of statues of amber ; where through eternal summer even the mountains refuse to don a girdle of cloud. . . .

" Mighty Omataianuku !
" Dark Avaava the Tall !

" Tall Outuutu !

" Shadow the way for us !

" Tower as the cocoa-palms before us !

" Bend ye as dreams above the slumberers !

" Make deeper the sleep of the sleepers !

" Sleep, ye crickets of the threshold ! Sleep, ye never reposing ants ! Sleep, ye shining beetles of the night !

" Winds, cease ye from whispering ! Restless grass, pause in thy rustling ! Leaves of the palms, be still ! Reeds of the water-ways, sway not ! Blue river, cease thy lipping of the banks !

" Slumber, ye beams of the house, ye posts, great and small, ye rafters and ridge-poles, thatchings of grass, woven work of reeds, windows bamboo-latticed, doors that squeak like ghosts, low-glimmering fires of sandal-wood, — slumber ye all !

" O Omataianuku !

" Tall Outuutu !

' Dark Avaava !

" Make shadowy the way for us !

" Tower as the cocoa-palms before us !

" Bend ye as dreams above the slumberers !

" Make deeper the sleep of the sleepers, —

" Deeper the sleep of the winds, —

" Deeper the sleep of the waters, —

" Dimmer the dimness of night !
" Veil ye the moon with your breathings !
" Make fainter the fires of the stars !
" In the name of the weird ones : —
" Omataianuku !
" Outuuturoraa !
" Ovaavaroroa !
" Sleep !
" Sleep ! "

***

So, with the rising of each new moon, was
heard the magical song of the thieves, — the first
night, low as the humming of the wind among
the cocoa-palms ; louder and louder each suc-
ceeding night, and clearer and sweeter, until the
great white face of the full moon flooded the
woods with light, and made silver pools about
the columns of the palms. For the magic of the
full moon was mightier than the witchcraft of the
song ; and the people of Rarotonga slept not.
But of other nights the invisible thieves did carry
away many cocoanuts and taros, and plantains
and bananas, despite the snares set for them by
the people of Rarotonga. And it was observed
with terror that cocoanuts were removed from
the crests of trees so lofty that no human hand
might have reached them.

***

But the chief Aki, being one night by the fountain Vaipiki, which gushes out from the place of waters that flow below the world, beheld rising up from the water, just as the thin moon looked into it, a youth and a girl whiter than the moon herself, naked as fishes, beautiful as dreams. And they began to sing a song, at whose sound Aki, hidden among the pandanus leaves, stopped his ears, — the wizard-song, *E tira Omataia-nuku, E tira Outuuturoroa!* And the winds were stilled, and the waves sank to sleep, and the palm-leaves ceased to nod, and the song of the crickets was hushed.

**

Then Aki, devising to capture them, set a great fish-net deep within the fountain, and waited for their return. The vast silence of the night deepened; the smoke of the mountain of fire, blood-tinted from below, hung motionless in the sky, like a giant's plume of feathers. At last the winds of the sea began their ghost whisperings among the palm-groves; a cricket chirped, and a million insect-chants responded; the new moon plunged one of her pale horns into the ocean; the east whitened and changed hue like the belly of a shark. The spell was broken, the day was dawning.

And Aki beheld the White Ones returning, bearing with them fruits and nuts and fragrant herbs. Rising suddenly from his hiding-place among the leaves, he rushed upon them; and they leaped into the fountain, like fishes, leaving their fruits scattered upon the brink. But, lo! they were caught in the net!

Then Aki strove to pull the net on shore; and, being a strong man, he easily moved it. But, in turning, the male leaped through the opening of the net, and flashed like a salmon through the deeps down to the unknown abyss of waters below, so that Aki caught the girl only. Vainly she struggled in the net; and her moon-white body took opalescent gleams, like the body of a beautiful fish in the hands of the captor. Vainly she wept and pleaded; and Aki blocked up the bottom of the fountain with huge blocks of coral, lest, slipping away from him, she might disappear again. But, looking upon the strangeness of her beauty, he kissed her and comforted her; and she ceased at last to weep. Her eyes were large and dark, like a tropical heaven flashed with stars.

..*

So it came to pass that Aki loved her; more than his own life he loved her. And the people wondered at her beauty; for light came from her

as she moved, and when she swam in the river
her passage was like the path of the moon on
waters, — a quivering column of brightness. Only,
it was noticed that this luminous beauty waxed
and waned contrariwise to the waxing and waning of the moon : her whiteness was whitest at
the time of the new moon ; it almost ceased to
glow when the face of the moon was full.   And
whensoever the new moon rose, she wept silently,
so that Aki could not comfort her, even after
having taught her the words of love in the tongue
of his own people, — the tongue, many-vowelled,
that wooes the listener like the mockery of a
night-bird's song.

.*.

Thus many years passed away, and Aki became old ; but she seemed ever the same, for the
strange race to which she belonged never grow
old.   Then it was noticed that her eyes became
deeper and sweeter, — weirdly sweet ; and Aki
knew that he would become a father in his age.
Yet she wept and pleaded with him, saying : —

"Lo! I am not of thy race, and at last I must
leave thee.   If thou lovest me, sever this white
body of mine, and save our child ; for if it suckle
me, I must dwell ten years longer in this world to
which I do not belong.   Thou canst not hurt mo

thus; for though I seem to die, yet my body will live on, — thou mayst not wound me more than water is wounded by axe or spear! For I am of the water and the light, of moonshine and of wind! And I may not suckle thy child.". . .

But Aki, fearing that he might lose both her and the child, pleaded with her successfully. And the child was beautiful as a white star, and she nursed it for ten happy years.

But, the ten years having passed, she kissed Aki, and said to him, "Alas! I must now leave thee, lest I die utterly; take thou away, therefore, the coral rocks from the fountain." And kissing him once more, she vowed to come back again, so that he complied at last with her request. She would have had him go with her; but he could not, being only mortal man. Then she passed away in the fountain deeps, like a gleam of light.

***

The child grew up very tall and beautiful, but not like his mother, — white only like strangers from beyond the sea. In his eyes there was, nevertheless, a strange light, brightest at the time of the new moon, waning with its waxing. . . . One night there came a great storm: the cocoa-palms bent like reeds, and a strange voice came with the wind, crying, calling! At dawn the white youth was gone, nor did human eyes ever behold him again.

But Aki lived beyond a hundred years, waiting for the return by the Vaipiki fountain, until his hair was whiter than the summer clouds. At last the people carried him away, and laid him in his house on a bed of pandanus leaves ; and all the women watched over him, lest he should die.

. . . It was the night of a new month, and the rising of the new moon. Suddenly a low sweet voice was heard, singing the old song that some remembered after the passing of half a hundred years. Sweeter and sweeter it grew ; higher rose the moon ! The crickets ceased to sing ; the cocoa-palms refused obeisance to the wind. And a heaviness fell upon the watchers, who, with open eyes, could move no limb, utter no voice. Then all were aware of a White Woman, whiter than moonlight, lithe-fashioned as a lake-fish, gliding between the ranks of the watchers ; and, taking Aki's gray head upon her bright breast, she sang to him, and kissed him, and stroked his aged face. . . .

The sun arose ; the watchers awakened. They bent over Aki, and it seemed that Aki slept lightly. But when they called him, he answered not ; when they touched him, he stirred not. He slept for-ever ! . . .

THE BIRD WIFE.

There the Moon becometh old and again young many times, as one that dieth often and is reanimated as often by enchantment; while the Sun moveth in a circle of pallid mists, and setteth not. But when he setteth at last, it is still light; for the dead make red fires in the sky above the icebergs until after many, many dim months he riseth again.

ALL things there are white, save the black sea and the wan fogs; and yet it is hard to discover where the water ends and the land begins, for that part of the world the gods forgot to finish. The ice-peaks grow and diminish, and shift their range northward and southward, and change their aspects grotesquely. There are Faces in the ice that lengthen and broaden; and Forms as of vanished creatures. When it is full moon the innumerable multitude of dogs, that live upon dead fish, howl all together at the roaring sea; and the great bears hearing huddle themselves together on the highest heights of the glaciers, and thence hurl down sharp white crags upon the dogs. Above all, rising into the Red Lights, there is a mountain which has been a fountain of living fire ever since the being of the world; and all the surface of the land about is heaped with monstrous bones. But this is summer in that place; in winter there is no sound but the groaning of the ice, the shrieking of the winds, the gnashing of the teeth of the floes.

Now there are men in those parts, whose houses are huts of snow, lighted by lamps fed with the oil of sea-creatures; and the wild dogs obey them. But they live in fear of the Havstramb, that monster which has the form of an armless man and the green color of ancient ice; they fear the Margige, shaped like a woman, which cries under the ice on which their huts repose; and the goblin Bear whose fangs are icicles; and the Kajarissat, which are the spirits of the icebergs, drawing the kayaks under the black water; and the ghostly ivory-hunter who drives his vapory and voiceless team over ice thinner than the scales of fish; and the white Spectre that lies in wait for those who lose their way by night, having power to destroy all whom he can excite to laughter by weird devices; and the white-eyed deer which must not be pursued. There also is the home of the warlocks, the wizards, the Iliseetsut, — creators of the Tupilek.

Now the Tupilek is of all awful things the most awful, of all unutterable things the most unutterable.

For that land is full of bones, — the bones of
sea monsters and of earth monsters, the skulls
and ribs of creatures that perished in eons ere
man was born ; and there are mountains, there
are islands, of these bones. Sometimes great merchants from far southern countries send thither
ivory-hunters with sledges and innumerable dogs
to risk their lives for those white teeth, those ter-
rific tusks, which protrude from the ice and from
the sand, that is not deep enough to cover them.
And the Ilisectsut seek out the hugest of these
bones, and wrap them in a great whale skin, together with the hearts and the brains of many
sea creatures and earth animals ; and they utter
strange words over them. Then the vast mass
quivers and groans and shapes itself into a form
more hideous, more enormous, than any form
created by the gods ; it moves upon many feet ;
it sees with many eyes ; it devours with innumerable teeth ; it obeys the will of its creator ;
it is a Tupilek !

**

And all things change form in that place, —
even as the ice shifts its shapes fantastically,
as the boundaries of the sand eternally vary,
as bone becomes earth and earth seems to become bone. So animals also take human like-

ness, birds assume human bodies; for there is
sorcery in all things there. Thus it came to pass,
one day, that a certain ivory-hunter beheld a
flock of sea-birds change themselves into women;
and creeping cautiously over the white snow —
himself being clad in white skins — he came
suddenly upon them, and caught hold of the
nearest one with a strong hand, while the rest,
turning again to birds, flew southward with long
weird screams.

Slender was the girl, like a young moon, and as
white; and her eyes black and soft, like those of
the wild gulls. So the hunter — finding that she
struggled not, but only wept — felt pity for her,
and, taking her into his warm hut of snow, clothed
her in soft skins and fed her with the heart of a
great fish. Then, his pity turning to love, she
became his wife.

Two years they lived thus together, and he fed
her with both fish and flesh, being skilful in the
use of the net and the bow; but always while
absent he blocked up the door of the hut, lest she
might change into a bird again, and so take wing.
After she had borne him two children, nevertheless, his fear passed from him, like the memory
of a dream; and she followed him to the chase,
managing the bow with wonderful skill. But she

prevailed upon him that he should not smite the wild gulls.

So they lived and so loved until the children became strong and swift.

Then it came to pass one day, while they were hunting all together, that many birds had been killed; and she called to the children, " Little ones, bring me quickly some feathers!" And they came to her with their hands full; and she laid the feathers upon their arms and upon her own shoulders, and shrieked to them, " Fly! ye are of the race of birds, ye are the Wind's children!"

Forthwith their garments fell from them; and, being changed into wild gulls, mother and children rose in the bright icy air, circling and circling, higher and higher, against the sky. Thrice above the weeping father they turned in spiral flight, thrice screamed above the peaks of glimmering ice, and, sweeping suddenly toward the far south, whirred away forever.

॥ॐ॥

TALES FROM INDIAN AND BUDDHIST LITERATURE.

THE MAKING OF TILOTTAMA.

Which is told of in the holy MAHABHARATA, *written by the blessed Richi Krishna-Dvaipayana, who composed it in twenty-four thousand slokas,[1] and who composed six millions of slokas likewise. Of the latter are three millions in the keeping of the gods; and one million five hundred thousand in the keeping of the Gandharbas, who are the musicians of Indra's Heaven; and one million four hundred thousand in the keeping of the Pitris, who are the ghosts of the blessed dead; and one hundred thousand in the keeping of men. . . . And the guiltiest of men who shall hear the recital of the* MAHABHARATA *shall be delivered from all his sins; neither sickness nor misfortune shall come nigh him.*

Now I shall tell you how it happened that the great gods once became multiple-faced and myriad-

[1] According to the exordium in the *Adi-Parva* of the Mahabharata, this now most gigantic of epics at first consisted of 24,000 slokas only. Subsequent additions swelled the number of its distiches to the prodigious figure of 107,389. — L. H.

eyed by reason of a woman's beauty, as the same is recounted in the Book of Great Weight, — in the Mahabharata.

* *

In ancient years there were two Daiteyas, twin brothers sprung from the race of the Asouras, the race of evil genii; and their names were Sounda and Oupasounda. Princes they were born; cruel and terrible they grew up, yet were ever one in purpose, in thought, in the pursuit of pleasure, or in the perpetration of crime.

And in the course of time it came to pass that the brothers resolved to obtain domination over the Three Worlds, and to practise all those austerities and sacrifices by which the holiest ascetics elevate themselves to divinity. So they departed to the solitude of the mountain Vindhya, and there devoted themselves to contemplations and to prayer, until their mighty limbs became slender as jungle-canes, and their joints like knots of bone. And they ceased all the actions of life, and forbore all contact with things earthly, — knowing that contact with earthly things begetteth sensation, and sensation desire, and desire corruption, and corruption existence. Thus by dint of meditation and austerity the world became for them as non-existent. By one effort of will they might have shaken the universe; the world trembled under the weight of their thoughts as though laboring in earthquake. Air was their only nourishment; they offered up their own flesh in sacrifice; and the Vindhya, heated by the force of their austerities, smoked to heaven like a mountain of fire.

Therefore the divinities, being terrified, sought to divert them from their austerities, and to trouble their senses by apparitions of women and of demons and of gods. But the Asouras ceased not a moment to practise their mortifications, standing upon their great toes only, and keeping their eyes fixed upon the sun.

..*

Now, after many years, it came to pass that Brahma, Ancient of Days, Father of the Creator of Worlds, appeared before them as a Shape of light, and bade them ask for whatsoever they desired. And they made answer, with hands joined before their foreheads: "If the Father of the Father of Worlds be gratified by our penances, we desire to acquire knowledge of all arts of magic and arts of war, to possess the gifts of beauty and of strength, and the promise of immortality."

But the Shape of Brahma answered unto them: "Immortality will not be given unto you, O

Princes of Daiteyas, inasmuch as ye practised
austerities only that ye might obtain dominion
over the Three Worlds. Yet will I grant ye the
knowledge and power and the bodily gifts ye desire. Also it shall be vouchsafed you that none
shall be able to destroy you ; neither among creatures of earth nor spirits nor gods shall any have
power to do you hurt, save ye hurt one another."

Thus the two Daiteyas obtained the favor of
Brahma, and became unconquerable by gods or
men. And they returned to their habitation, and
departed utterly from the path of righteousness,
eating and drinking and sinning exceedingly,
more than any of their evil race had done before
them ; so that their existence might be likened to
one never-ending feast of unholy pleasures. But
no pleasures could satiate these Asouras, though
all mortals dwelling with them suffered by reason
of monstrous excesses.

By the two Daiteyas, indeed, repose and sleep
were never desired nor even needed, — night and
day were as one for them ; but those mortals
about them speedily died of pleasure, and the
Daiteyas were angry with them because they died.

* * *

Now, at last, the two Asouras resolved to
forego pleasure awhile, that they might make

the conquest of the Three Worlds by force of that magical knowledge imparted to them by will of Brahma. And they warred against Indra's Heaven; for it had been given them to move through air more swiftly than demons. The Souras, indeed, and the gods knowing of their coming and the nature of the powers that had been given them, passed away to the Brahmaloka, where dwell the spirits of the holiest dead. But the Daiteyas, taking possession with their army of evil genii, slew many of the Yakshas, who are the guardians of treasures, and the Rakshas, which are demons, and multitudes of all the beings which fly through the airs. After these things they slew all the Nagas, the human-visaged serpents living in the entrails of the world; and they overcame all the creatures of the sea.

Then they made resolve to extend their evil power over the whole earth, and to destroy all worshippers of the gods. For the prayers and the sacrifices offered up by the Radjarchis and the Brahmans continually augmented the power of the gods; and these Daiteyas therefore hated exceedingly all holy men. Because of the power given the wicked princes, none could oppose their will, nor did the mighty imprecations of the hermits and the Brahmans avail. All worshippers of the gods were destroyed; the eternal altar-fires were scattered and extinguished; the holy offerings were cast into the waters; the sacred vessels were broken; the awful temples were cast down; and the face of the earth made vast with desolation, as though ravaged by the god of death. And the Asouras, changing themselves by magical art into the form of tigers, of lions, of furious elephants, sought out all those ascetics who lived in the secret hollows of the mountains or the unknown recesses of the forest or the deep silence of the jungles, and destroyed them. So that the world became a waste strewn with human bones; and there were no cities, no populations, no smoke of sacrifice, no murmur of prayer, no human utterance, — vast horror only, and hideous death.

***

Then all the holy people of air, — the Siddhas and the Devarchis and the Paramarchis, — aghast at the desolation of the world. and filled with divinest compassion for the universe, flocked to the dwelling-place of Brahma, and made plaint to him of these things which had been done. and besought him that he would destroy the power of Sounda and Oupasounda. Now Brahma was seated among the gods, surrounded by the circles

of the Siddhas and the Bramarchis; Mahadeva
was there, and Indra, and Agni, Prince of Fire,
and Vayou, Lord of Winds, and Aditaya, the Sun-
god, who drives the seven-headed steeds, and
Tchandra, the lotos-loving god of the Moon. And
all the elders of heaven stood about them, — the
holy Marichipas and Adjas and Avimoudhas and
Tedjogharbas; the Vanaprasthas of the forest,
and the Siddhas of the airs, and the Vaikhanas
who live upon roots, and the sixty thousand luminous Balakhilyas, — not bigger than the thumb of
a man, — who sprang from the hairs of Brahma.

Then from the violet deeps of the eternities
Brahma summoned unto him Viswakarman, the
Fashioner of the Universe, the Creator of Worlds,
— Viswakarman, Kindler of all the Lights of
Heaven. And Viswakarman arose from the eter-
nities as a star-cloud, and stood in light before
the All-Father.

And Brahma spake unto him, saying : " O
my golden son, O Viswakarman, create me a
woman fairer than the fairest, sweeter than the
sweetest, — whose beauty might even draw the
hearts of all divinities, as the moon draweth all
the waters in her train. . . . I wait ! "

***

So Viswakarman, veiling himself in mists,

wrought in obedience to the Father of Gods, invisibly, awfully, with all manner of precious gems, with all colors of heaven, with all perfume of flowers, with all rays of light, with all tones of music, with all things beautiful and precious to the sight, to the touch, to the hearing, to the taste, to the sense of odors. And as vapors are wrought into leafiest lacework of frosts, as sunbeams are transmuted into gems of a hundred colors, so, all mysteriously, were ten thousand priceless things blended into one new substance of life; and the substance found shape, and was resolved into the body of a woman. All blossom-beauty tempted in her bosom; all perfume lingered in her breath; all jewel-fires made splendor for her eyes; her locks were wrought of sunlight and of gold; the flowers of heaven rebudded in her lips; the pearl and the fairy opal blended in her smile; the tones of her voice were made with the love-songs of a thousand birds. And a name was given unto her, Tilottama, which signifies in that ancient Indian tongue, spoken of gods and men, " Fair-wrought of daintiest atoms." . . . Then Viswakarman passed away as the glory of evening fades out, and sank into the Immensities, and mingled with the Eternities where no time or space is.

.*.

And Tilottama, clothed only with light as with a garment, joining her hands before her luminous brows in adoration, bowed down to the Father of Gods, and spake with the sweetest voice ever heard even within the heaven of heavens, saying : " O thou universal Father, let me know thy will, and the divine purpose for which I have been created."

And the deep tones of gold made answer, gently : "Descend, good Tilottama, into the world of men, and display the witchcraft of thy beauty in the sight of Sounda and Oupasounda, so that the Daiteyas may be filled with hatred, each against the other, because of thee."

" It shall be according to thy desire, O Master of Creatures," answered Tilottama ; and, having prostrated her beautiful body thrice before Brahma, she glided about the circle of the gods, saluting all as she passed.

Now the great god Siva, the blessed Maheswara, was seated in the south, with face turned toward the east ; the other gods were looking toward the north ; and the seven orders of the richis — the Devarchis, Bramarchis, Maharchis, Paramarchis, Radjarchis, Kandarchis, and Sroutarchis — sat upon every side. And while Tilottama passed around the circle, the gods strove not to gaze upon her, lest their hearts should be drawn irresistibly toward that magical beauty, created not for joy, indeed, but verily for destruction. So for a moment Indra and the blessed Sthanou made their hearts strong against her. But as she drew near to Maheswara, who kept his face to the east, there came to Maheswara another face, a face upon the south side, with eyes more beautiful than lotos-flowers. And when she turned behind him, there came to him yet another face upon the west side; and even as she turned to the north, there came to him a face upon the north side, so that he could not choose but gaze upon her. And even great Indra's body, as she turned around him, blossomed with eyes, before, behind, on every side, even to the number of a thousand eyes, large and deep and ruddy-lidded. Thus it was that Mahadeva became the Four-faced God, and Balasoudana the God with a Thousand Eyes. And new faces grew upon all the divinities and all habitants of heaven as Tilottama passed around them; all became double-faced, triple-faced, or myriad-faced, in despite of their purpose not to look upon her, so mighty was the magic of her loveliness! Only Brahma, Father of all the Gods, remained impassive as eternity; for unto him beauty and hideousness,

light and darkness, night and day, death and life,
the finite and the infinite, are ever one and the
same. . . .

**

Now Sounda and Oupasounda were diverting
themselves with their wicked women among the
mountains, when they first perceived Tilottama
gathering flowers ; and at the sight of her their
hearts ceased to pulsate. And they forgot not
only all that they had done, and their riches and
their power and their pleasures, but also the divine provision that they could die only by each
other's hands. Each drew near unto Tilottama ;
each sought to kiss her mouth ; each repulsed his
brother ; each claimed her for himself. And the
first hatred of each other made flame in their
eyes. " Mine she shall be ! " cried Oupasounda.
" Wrest her from me if thou canst ! " roared
Sounda in mad defiance. And passing from
words to reproaches, and from reproaches to
mighty blows, they fell upon each other with
their weapons, and strove together until both
were slain.

Then a great fear came upon all the evil company, and the women fled shrieking away ; and
the Asouras, beholding the hand of Brahma in
these things, trembled, and took flight, return-

ing unto their abode of fire and darkness, even unto the Patala, which is the habitation of the damned.

*

But Tilottama, returning to the Brahmaloka, received the commendation of the gods, and kindly praise from Brahma, Father of Worlds and Men, who bade her ask for whatsoever grace she most desired. But she asked him only that she might dwell forever in that world of splendors and of light, which the blessed inhabit. And the Universal Father made answer, saying: " Granted is thy prayer, O most seductive among created beings! thou shalt dwell in the neighborhood of the sun, yet not among the gods, lest mischief be wrought. And the dazzle of thy beauty shall hinder the eyes of mortals from beholding thee, that their hearts be not consumed because of thee. Dwell therefore within the heaven of the sun forevermore."

And Brahma, having restored to Indra the dominion of the Three Worlds, withdrew into the infinite light of the Brahmaloka.

THE BRAHMAN AND HIS BRAHMANI.

*The wise will not attach themselves unto women ; for women
sport with the hearts of those who love them, even as with
ravens whose wing-feathers have been plucked out. . . . There
is honey in the tongues of women ; there is nought in their
heart save the venom halahala. . . . Their nature is mobile as
the eddies of the sea ; their affection endures no longer than the
glow of gold above the place of sunset : all venom within, all
fair without, women are like unto the fruit of the goundja.
. . . Therefore the experienced and wise do avoid women, even
as they shun the water-vessels that are placed within the ceme-
teries. . . .*

In the "Pantchopakhyana," and also in that
"Ocean of the Rivers of Legend," which is
called in the ancient Indian tongue "Kathasa-
ritsagara," may be found this story of a Brahman
and his Brahmani : —

. . . Never did the light that is in the eyes
of lovers shine more tenderly than in the eyes
of the Brahman who gave his life for the life of
the woman under whose lotos-feet he laid his
heart. Yet what man lives that hath not once
in his time been a prey to the madness inspired
by woman ? . . .

He alone loved her; his family being loath to endure her presence, — for in her tongue was the subtle poison that excites sister against brother, friend against friend. But so much did he love her that for her sake he abandoned father and mother, brother and sister, and departed with his Brahmani to seek fortune in other parts. Happily his guardian Deva accompanied him, — for he was indeed a holy man, having no fault but the folly of loving too much; and the Deva, by reason of spiritual sight, foresaw all that would come to pass.

As they were journeying together through the elephant-haunted forest, the young woman said to her husband: " O thou son of a venerable man, thy Brahmani dies of thirst; fetch her, she humbly prays thee, a little water from the nearest spring." And the Brahman forthwith hastened to the running brook, with the gourd in his hand; but when he had returned with the water, he found his beloved lying dead upon a heap of leaves. Now this death was indeed the unseen work of the good Deva.

So, casting the gourd from him, the Brahman burst into tears, and sobbed as though his soul would pass from him, and kissed the beautiful dead face and the slender dead feet and the

golden throat of his Brahmani, shrieking betimes
in his misery, and daring to question the gods as
to why they had so afflicted him. But even as he
lamented, a voice answered him in syllables clear
as the notes of a singing bird: "Foolish man!
wilt thou give half of thy life in order that thy
Brahmani shall live again?"

And he, in whom love had slain all fear, answered untremblingly to the Invisible: "Yea,
O Narayana, half of my life will I give unto her
gladly." Then spake the Invisible: "Foolish
man! pronounce the three mystic syllables."
And he pronounced them; and the Brahmani,
as if awaking from a dream, unclosed her jewel-
eyes, and wound her round arms about her husband's neck, and with her fresh lips drank the
rain of his tears as the lips of a blossom drink in
the dews of the night.

* *

So, having eaten of fruits and refreshed themselves, both proceeded upon their way; and at
last, leaving the forest, they came to a great
stretch of gardens lying without a white city, —
gardens rainbow-colored with flowers of marvellous perfume, and made cool by fountains flowing from the lips of gods in stone and from the
trunks of elephants of rock. Then said the

loving husband to his Brahmani: " Remain here
a little while, thou too sweet one, that I may
hasten on to return to thee sooner with fruits
and refreshing drink.". . .

Now in that place of gardens dwelt a youth,
employed to draw up water by the turning of a
great wheel, and to cleanse the mouths of the
fountains; and although a youth, he had been
long consumed by one of those maladies that
make men tremble with cold beneath a sky of
fire, so that there was little of his youthfulness
left to him excepting his voice. But with that
voice he charmed the hearts of women, as the
juggler charms the hooded serpent; and, seeing
the wife of the Brahman, he sang that she might
hear.

He sang as the birds sing in the woods in pair-
ing time, as the waters sing that lip the curves of
summered banks, as the Apsaras sang in other kal-
pas; and he sang the songs of Amarou, — Amarou, sweetest of all singers, whose soul had passed
through a century of transmigrations in the bodies of a hundred fairest women, until he became
the world's master in all mysteries of love. And
as the Brahmani listened, Kama transpierced her
heart with his flower-pointed arrows, so that. ap-
proaching the youth, she pressed her lips upon

his lips, and murmured, " If thou lovest me not,
I die."

***

Therefore, when the Brahman returned with
fruits and drink, she coaxed him that he should
share these with the youth, and even prayed him
that he should bring the youth along as a travelling companion or as a domestic.

"Behold!" answered the Brahman, "this young
man is too feeble to bear hardship; and if he fall
by the wayside, I shall not be strong enough to
carry him." But the Brahmani answered, " Nay!
should he fall, then will I myself carry him in my
basket, upon my head;" and the Brahman yielded
to her request, although marvelling exceedingly.
So they all travelled on together.

Now one day, as they were reposing by a deep
well, the Brahmani, beholding her husband asleep,
pushed him so that he fell into the well; and she
departed, taking the youth with her. Soon after
this had happened, they came to a great city where
a famous and holy king lived, who loved all Brahmans and had built them a temple surrounded by
rich lands, paying for the land by laying golden
elephant-feet in lines round about it. And the
cunning Brahmani, when arrested by the toll-
collectors and taken before this king, — still

5

bearing the sick youth upon her head in a basket,
— boldly spake to the king, saying: " This, most
holy of kings, is my dearest husband, a righteous
Brahman, who has met with affliction while per-
forming the good works ordained for such as he ;
and inasmuch as heirs sought his life, I have concealed him in this basket and brought him hither."
Then the king, being filled with compassion, be-
stowed upon the Brahmani and her pretended husband the revenues of two villages and the freedom
thereof, saying: " Thou shalt be henceforth as my
sister, thou comeliest and truest of women."

**

But the poor Brahman was not dead ; for his
good Deva had preserved his life within the well-
pit, and certain travellers passing by drew him
up and gave him to eat.   Thus it happened that
he presently came to the same village in which
the wicked Brahmani dwelt ; and, fearing with an
exceeding great fear, she hastened to the king,
and said, " Lo ! the enemy who seeketh to kill my
husband pursueth after us."

Then said the king, " Let him be trampled
under foot by the elephants ! "

But the Brahman, struggling in the grasp of
the king's men, cried out, with a bitter cry : " O
king ! art thou indeed called just, who will not

hearken to the voice of the accused? This fair but wicked woman is indeed my own wife; ere I be condemned, let her first give back to me that which I gave her!"

And the king bade his men stay their hands. "Give him back," he commanded, in a voice of tempest, "that which belongs to him!"

But the Brahmani protested, saying, "My lord, I have nought which belongs to him." So the king's brow darkened with the frown of a maharajah.

"Give me back," cried the Brahman, "the life which I gave thee, my own life given to thee with the utterance of the three mystic syllables, — the half of my own years."

Then, through exceeding fear of the king, she murmured, "Yea, I render it up to thee, the life thou gavest me with the utterance of the three mystic syllables," — and fell dead at the king's feet.

Thus the truth was made manifest; and hence the proverb arose: —

"*She for whom I gave up family, home, and even the half of my life, hath abandoned me, the heartless one! What man may put faith in women!*"

BAKAWALI.

There is in the Hindustani language a marvellous tale written by a Moslem, but treating nevertheless of the ancient gods of India, and of the Apsaras and of the Rakshasas. " The Rose of Bakawali" it is called. Therein also may be found many strange histories of fountains filled with magical waters, changing the sex of those who bathe therein ; and histories of flowers created by witchcraft — never fading — whose perfumes give sight to the blind ; and, above all, this history of love human and superhuman, for which a parallel may not be found. . . .

. . In days when the great Rajah Zain-ulmuluk reigned over the eastern kingdoms of Hindostan, it came to pass that Bakawali, the Apsara, fell in love with a mortal youth who was none other than the son of the Rajah. For the lad was beautiful as a girl, beautiful even as the god Kama, and seemingly created for love. Now in that land all living things are sensitive to loveliness, even the plants themselves, — like the Asoka that bursts into odorous blossom when touched even by the foot of a comely maiden. Yet was Bakawali fairer than any earthly creature, being a daughter of the immortals ; and those who had seen her, believing her born of mortal woman, would answer when interrogated concerning her, " Ask not us !

rather ask thou the nightingale to sing of her beauty."

Never had the youth Taj-ulmuluk guessed that his beloved was not of mortal race, having encountered her as by hazard, and being secretly united to her after the Gandharva fashion. But he knew that her eyes were preternaturally large and dark, and the odor of her hair like Tartary musk; and there seemed to transpire from her when she moved such a light and such a perfume that he remained bereft of utterance, while watching her, and immobile as a figure painted upon a wall. And the lamp of love being enkindled in the heart of Bakawali, her wisdom, like a golden moth, consumed itself in the flame thereof, so that she forgot her people utterly, and her immortality, and even the courts of heaven wherein she was wont to dwell.

* *

In the sacred books of the Hindus there is much written concerning the eternal city Amar-nagar, whose inhabitants are immortal. There Indra, azure-bearded, dwells in sleepless pleasure, surrounded by his never-slumbering court of celestial bayaderes, circling about him as the constellations of heaven circle in their golden dance about Surya, the sun. And this was Bakawali's home, that she had abandoned for the love of a man.

So it came to pass one night, a night of perfume and of pleasure, that Indra started up from his couch like one suddenly remembering a thing long forgotten, and asked of those about him : " How happens it that Bakawali, daughter of Firoz, no more appears before us?" And one of them made answer, saying : "O great Indra, that pretty fish hath been caught in the net of human love! Like the nightingale, never does she cease to complain because it is not possible for her to love even more ; intoxicated is she with the perishable youth and beauty of her mortal lover; and she lives only for him and in him, so that even her own kindred are now forgotten or have become to her objects of aversion. And it is because of him, O Lord of Suras and Devas, that the rosy one no longer presents herself before thy court."

Then was Indra wroth ; and he commanded that Bakawali be perforce brought before him, **that** she might render account of her amorous folly. And the Devas, awaking her, placed her in their cloud-chariot, and brought her into the presence of Indra, her lips still humid with mortal kisses, and on her throat red-blossom marks left by human lips. And she knelt before him, with fingers joined as in prayer; while the Lord of the firmament gazed at her in silent anger, with such a frown as he was wont to wear when riding to battle upon his elephant triple-trunked. Then said he to the Devas about him: " Let her be purified by fire, inasmuch as I discern about her an odor of mortality offensive to immortal sense. And even so often as she returns to her folly, so often let her be consumed in my sight." . . .

Accordingly they bound the fairest of Apsaras, and cast her into a furnace furious as the fires of the sun, so that within a moment her body was changed to a white heap of ashes. But over the ashes was magical water sprinkled; and out of the furnace Bakawali arose, nude as one newly born, but more perfect in rosy beauty even than before. And Indra commanded her to dance before him, as she was wont to do in other days.

So she danced all those dances known in the courts of heaven, curving herself as flowers curve under a perfumed breeze, as water serpentines under the light; and she circled before them rapidly as a leaf-whirling wind, lightly as a bee, with myriad variations of delirious grace, with ever-shifting enchantment of motion, until the hearts

of all who looked upon her were beneath those
shining feet, and all cried aloud : " O flower-
body! O rose-body! O marvel of the Garden
of Grace ! blossom of daintiness ! O flower-
body ! "

* * *

Thus was she each night obliged to appear before Indra at Armanagar, and each night to suffer
the fiercest purification of fire, forasmuch as she
would not forsake her folly ; and each night also
did she return to her mortal lover, and take her
wonted place beside him without awaking him,
having first bathed her in the great fountain of
rosewater within the court.

But once it happened that Taj-ulmuluk awoke
in the night, and reaching out his arms found she
was not there.   Only the perfume of her head
upon the pillow, and odorous garments flung in
charming formlessness upon every divan. . . .

When she returned, seemingly fairer than before, the youth uttered no reproach, but on the
night following he slit up the tip of his finger
with a sharp knife, and filled the wound with salt
that he might not sleep.   Then, when the aerial
chariot descended all noiselessly, like some long
cloud moon-silvered, he arose and followed Bakawali unperceived.   Clinging underneath the char-

iot, he was borne above winds even to Armanagar, and into the jewelled courts and into the presence of Indra. But Indra knew not, for his senses were dizzy with sights of beauty and the fumes of soma-wine.

Then did Taj-ulmuluk, standing in the shadow of a pillar, behold beauty such as he had never before seen — save in Bakawali — and hear music sweeter than mortal musician may ever learn. Splendors bewildered his eyes; and the crossing of the fretted and jewelled archwork above him seemed an intercrossing and interblending of innumerable rainbows. But when it was given to him, all unexpectedly, to view the awful purification of Bakawali, his heart felt like ice within him, and he shrieked. Nor could he have refrained from casting himself also into that burst of white fire, had not the magical words been pronounced and the wizard-water sprinkled before he was able to move a limb. Then did he behold Bakawali rising from her snowy cinders, — shining like an image of the goddess Lakshmi in the fairest of her thousand forms, — more radiant than before, like some comet returning from the embraces of the sun with brighter curves of form and longer glories of luminous hair. . . .

And Bakawali danced and departed, Taj-

ulmuluk likewise returning even as he had
come. . . .

* *

But when he told her, in the dawn of the morning, that he had accompanied her in her voyage
and had surprised her secret, Bakawali wept and
trembled for fear. " Alas! alas! what hast thou
done?" she sobbed; "thou hast become thine
own greatest enemy. Never canst thou know all
that I have suffered for thy sake, — the maledic-
tions of my kindred, the insults of all belonging
to my race. Yet rather than turn away my face
from thy love, I suffered nightly the agonies of
burning; I have died a myriad deaths rather than
lose thee. Thou hast seen it with thine own
eyes! . . . But none of mankind may visit unbid-
den the dwelling of the gods and return with im-
punity. Now, alas! the evil hath been done;
nor can I devise any plan by which to avert thy
danger, save that of bringing thee again secretly
to Armanagar and charming Indra in such wise
that he may pardon all.". . .

* *

So Bakawali the Apsara suffered once more the
agony of fire, and danced before the gods, not only
as she had danced before, but so that the eyes
of all beholding her became dim in watching the

varying curves of her limbs, the dizzy speed of
her white feet, the tossing light of her hair. And
the charm of her beauty bewitched the tongues of
all there, so that the cry, "O flower-body!"
fainted into indistinguishable whispers, and the
fingers of the musicians were numbed with lan-
guor, and the music weakened tremblingly, quiv-
eringly, dying down into an amorous swoon.

And out of the great silence broke the soft
thunder of Indra's pleased voice: "O Bakawali!
ask me for whatever thou wilt, and it shall be
accorded thee. By the Trimurti, I swear!"...
But she, kneeling before him, with bosom still
fluttering from the dance, murmured: "I pray
thee, divine One, only that thou wilt allow me
to depart hence, and dwell with this mortal whom
I love during all the years of life allotted unto
him." And she gazed upon the youth Taj-
ulmuluk.

But Indra, hearing these words, and looking
also at Taj-ulmuluk, frowned so darkly that
gloom filled all the courts of heaven. And he
said: "Thou, also, son of man, wouldst doubtless
make the same prayer; yet think not thou mayst
take hence an Apsara like Bakawali to make her
thy wife without grief to thyself! And as for
thee, O shameless Bakawali, thou mayst depart

with him, indeed, since I have sworn; but I swear
also to thee that from thy waist unto thy feet thou
shalt remain a woman of marble for the space of
twelve years. . . . Now let thy lover rejoice in
thee!". . .

***

. . . And Bakawali was placed in the chamber
of a ruined pagoda, deep-buried within the forests
of Ceylon; and there did she pass the years, sitting upon a seat of stone, herself stone from feet
to waist. But Taj-ulmuluk found her and ministered unto her as to the statue of a goddess; and
he waited for her through the long years.

The ruined pavement, grass-disjointed, trembled to the passing tread of wild elephants; often
did tigers peer through the pillared entrance, with
eyes flaming like emeralds; but Taj-ulmuluk was
never weary nor afraid, and he waited by her
through all the weary and fearful years.

Gem-eyed lizards clung and wondered; serpents
watched with marvellous chrysolite gaze; vast
spiders wove their silvered lace above the head
of the human statue; sunset-feathered birds, with
huge and flesh-colored beaks, hatched their young
in peace under the eyes of Bakawali. . . . Until
it came to pass at the close of the eleventh year,
— Taj-ulmuluk being in search of food, — that

the great ruin fell, burying the helpless Apsara under a ponderous and monstrous destruction beyond the power of any single arm to remove. . . . Then Taj-ulmuluk wept; but he still waited, knowing that the immortals could not die.

And out of the shapeless mass of ruins there soon grew a marvellous tree, graceful, dainty, round-limbed like a woman; and Taj-ulmuluk watched it waxing tall under the mighty heat of the summer, bearing flowers lovelier than that narcissus whose blossoms have been compared to the eyes of Oriental girls, and rosy fruit as smooth-skinned as maiden flesh.

So the twelfth year passed. And with the passing of its last moon, a great fruit parted itself, and therefrom issued the body of a woman, slender and exquisite, whose supple limbs had been folded up within the fruit as a butterfly is folded up within its chrysalis, comely as an Indian dawn, deeper-eyed than ever woman of earth, — being indeed an immortal, being an Apsara, — Bakawali reincarnated for her lover, and relieved from the malediction of the gods.

NATALIKA.

The story of a statue of sable stone among the ruins of Tirou-
vicaray, which are in the Land of Golconda that was. . . . When
the body shall have mouldered even as the trunk of a dead tree,
shall have crumbled to dust even as a clod of earth, the lovers of
the dead will turn away their faces and depart; but Virtue, re-
maining faithful, will lead the soul beyond the darknesses. . . .

THE yellow jungle-grasses are in the streets of
the city; the hooded serpents are coiled about
the marble legs of the gods. Bats suckle their
young within the ears of the granite elephants;
and the hairy spider spins her web for ruby-
throated humming-birds within the chambers of
kings. The pythons breed within the sanctuaries,
once ornate as the love-songs of Indian poets;
the diamond eyes of the gods have been plucked
out; lizards nestle in the lips of Siva; the centi-
pedes writhe among the friezes; the droppings of
birds whiten the altars. . . . But the sacred gate-
way of a temple still stands, as though preserved
by the holiness of its inscriptions: "The Self-
existent is not of the universe. . . . Man may not
take with him aught of his possessions beyond the
grave; let him increase the greatness of his good

deeds, even as the white ants do increase the height of their habitation. For neither father nor mother, neither sister nor brother, neither son nor wife, may accompany him to the other world; but Virtue only may be his comrade." . . . And these words, graven upon the stone, have survived the wreck of a thousand years.

*
* *

Now, among the broken limbs of the gods, and the jungle grasses, and the monstrous creeping plants that seem striving to strangle the elephants of stone, a learned traveller wandering in recent years came upon the statue of a maiden, in black granite, marvellously wrought. Her figure was nude and supple as those of the women of Krishna; on her head was the tiara of a princess, and from her joined hands escaped a cascade of flowers to fall upon the tablet supporting her exquisite feet. And on the tablet was the name NATALIKA; and above it a verse from the holy Ramayana, which signifies, in our tongue, these words: —

". . . *For I have been witness of this marvel, that by crushing the flowers in her hands, she made them to exhale a sweeter perfume.*"

*
* *

And this is the story of Natalika, as it is

told in the chronicle of the Moslem historian
Ferista : —

More than a thousand years ago there was war
between the Khalif Oualed and Dir-Rajah, of the
Kingdom of Sindh. The Arab horsemen swept
over the land like a typhoon ; and their eagle-
visaged hordes reddened the rivers with blood,
and made the nights crimson with the burning of
cities. Brahmanabad they consumed with fire,
and Alan and Dinal, making captives of the
women, and putting all males to the edge of
the scimitar. The Rajah fought stoutly for his
people and for his gods ; but the Arabs prevailed,
fearing nothing, remembering the words of the
Prophet, that " Paradise may be found in the
shadow of the crossing of swords." And at
Brahmanabad, Kassim, the zealous lieutenant of
the Khalif, captured the daughter of the Rajah,
and slew the Rajah and all his people.

* *

Her name was Natalika. When Kassim saw
her, fairer than that Love-goddess born from a
lotos-flower, her eyes softer than dew, her figure
lithe as reeds, her blue-black tresses rippling to
the gold rings upon her ankles, — he swore by the
Prophet's beard that she was the comeliest ever
born of woman, and that none should have her

save the Khalif Oualed. So he commanded that a troop of picked horsemen should take her to Bagdad, with much costly booty, — jewelry delicate and light as feathers, ivory carving miraculously wrought (sculptured balls within sculptured balls), emeralds and turquoises, diamonds and rubies, woofs of cashmere, and elephants, and dromedaries. And whosoever might do hurt to Natalika by the way, would have to pay for it with his head, as surely as the words of the Koran were the words of God's Prophet.

* * *

When Natalika came into the presence of the Khalif of Bagdad, the Commander of the Faithful could at first scarcely believe his eyes, seeing so beautiful a maiden; and starting from his throne without so much as looking at the elephants and the jewels and the slaves and the other gifts of Kassim, he raised the girl from her knees and kissed her in the presence of all the people, vowing that it rather behooved him to kneel before her than her to kneel before him. But she only wept, and answered not. . . .

And before many days the Khalif bade her know that he desired to make her his favorite wife; for since his eyes had first beheld her he could neither eat nor sleep for thinking of her.

6

Therefore he prayed that she would cease her
weeping, inasmuch as he would do more to make
her happy than any other might do, save only the
Prophet in his paradise.

Then Natalika wept more bitterly than before,
and vowed herself unworthy to be the bride of
the Khalif, although herself a king's daughter;
for Kassim had done her a grievous wrong ere
sending her to Bagdad. . . .

* *

Oualed heard the tale, and his mustaches curled
with wrath.   He sent his swiftest messengers
to India with a sealed parchment containing orders that Kassim should leave the land of Sindh
forthwith and hasten to Bassora, there to await
further commands.   Natalika shut herself up
alone in her chamber to weep; and the Khalif
wondered that he could not comfort her.   But
Kassim, leaving Sindh, wondered much more why
the Commander of the Faithful should have re-
called him, notwithstanding the beauty of the
gifts, the loveliness of the captives, the splendor
of the elephants.   Still marvelling, he rode into
Bassora, and sought the governor of that place.
Even while he was complaining there came forth
mutes with bow-strings, and they strangled Kassim
at the governor's feet.

* *

Days went and came; and at last there rode into Bagdad a troop of fierce horsemen, to the Khalif's palace. Their leader, advancing into Oualed's presence, saluted him, and laid at his feet a ghastly head with blood-bedabbled beard, the head of the great captain, Kassim.

**

"Lo!" cried Oualed to Natalika, "I have avenged thy wrong; and now, I trust, thou wilt believe that I love thee, and truly desire to set thee over my household as my wife, my queen, my sweetly beloved!"

But Natalika commenced to laugh with a wild and terrible laugh. "Know, O deluded one," she cried, "that Kassim was wholly innocent in that whereof I accused him, and that I sought only to avenge the death of my people, the murder of my brothers and sisters, the pillage of our homes, the sacrilegious destruction of the holy city Brahmanabad. Never shall I, the daughter of a Kshatrya king, ally myself with one of thy blood and creed. I have lived so long only that I might be avenged; and now that I am doubly avenged, by the death of our enemy, by thy hopeless dream of love for me, I die!" Piercing her bosom with a poniard, she fell at the Khalif's feet.

**

But Natalika's betrothed lover, Odayah-Rajah, avenged her even more, driving the circumcised conquerors from the land, and slaughtering all who fell into his hands. And the cruelties they had wrought he repaid them a hundred-fold.

Yet, growing weary of life by reason of Natalika's death, he would not reign upon the throne to which he had hoped to lift her in the embrace of love; but, retiring from the world, he became a holy mendicant of the temple of Tirouvicaray. . . .

And at last, feeling his end near, he dug himself a little grave under the walls of the temple; and ordered the most skilful sculptors to make the marble statue of his beloved, and that the statue should be placed upon his grave. Thus they wrought Natalika's statue as the statues of goddesses are wrought, but always according to his command, so that she seemeth to be crushing roses in her fingers. And when Odayah-Rajah passed away, they placed the statue of Natalika above him, so that her feet rest upon his heart.

"I have been witness of this marvel, that by crushing the flowers within her hands she made them to exhale a sweeter perfume!"

Were not those flowers the blossoming of her

beautiful youth, made lovelier by its own sacrifice?

The temple and its ten thousand priests are gone. But even after the lapse of a thousand years a perfume still exhales from those roses of stone!

THE CORPSE-DEMON.

There is a book written in the ancient tongue of India, and called VETALAPANTCHAVINSATI, *signifying " The Twenty-five Tales of a Demon.". . . And these tales are marvellous above all stories told by men; for wondrous are the words of Demons, and everlasting. . . . Now this Demon dwelt within a corpse, and spake with the tongue of the corpse, and gazed with the eyes of the corpse. And the corpse was suspended by its feet from a tree overshadowing tombs. . . .*

Now on the fourteenth of the moonless half of the month Bhadon, the Kshatrya king Vikramaditya was commanded by a designing Yogi that he should cut down the corpse and bring the same to him. For the Yogi thus designed to destroy the king in the night. . . .

And when the king cut down the corpse, the Demon which was in the corpse laughed and said: " If thou shouldst speak once upon the way, I go not with thee, but return unto my tree." Then the Demon began to tell to the king stories so strange that he could not but listen. And at the end of each story the Demon would ask hard questions, threatening to devour Vikramaditya should he not answer; and the king, rightly answering, indeed avoided destruction, yet, by speaking, perforce enabled the Demon to return to the tree. . . . Now listen to one of those tales which the Demon told : —

O KING, there once was a city called Dharmpur, whose rajah Dharmshil built a glorious temple to Devi, the goddess with a thousand shapes and a thousand names. In marble was the statue of the goddess wrought, so that she appeared seated cross-legged upon the cup of a monstrous lotos, two of her four hands being joined in prayer, and the other two uplifting on either side of her fountain basins, in each of which stood an elephant spouting perfumed spray. And there was exceeding great devotion at this temple ; and the people never wearied of presenting to the goddess sandal-wood, unbroken rice, consecrated food, flowers, and lamps burning odorous oil.

Now from a certain city there came one day in pilgrimage to Devi's temple, a washerman and a friend with him. Even as he was ascending the steps of the temple, he beheld a damsel descending toward him, unrobed above the hips, after the fashion of her people. Sweet as the moon was her face ; her hair was like a beautiful dark cloud ; her eyes were liquid and large as a wild deer's ; her brows were arched like bows well bent ; her delicate nose was curved like a falcon's beak; her neck was comely as a dove's; her teeth were like pomegranate seeds; her lips ruddy as the crimson gourd; her hands and feet soft as lotos-leaves. Golden-yellow was her skin, like the petals of the champa-flowers; and the pilgrim saw that she was graceful-waisted as a leopard. And while the tinkling of the gold rings about her round ankles receded beyond his hearing, his sight became dim for love, and he prayed his friend to discover for him who the maiden might be. . . . Now she was the daughter of a washerman.

Then did the pilgrim enter into the presence of the goddess, having his mind filled wholly by the vision of that girl; and prostrating himself he vowed a strange vow, saying: "O Devi, Mahadevi, — Mother of Gods and Monster-slayer, — before whom all the divinities bow down, thou hast delivered the earth from its burdens! thou hast delivered those that worshipped thee from a thousand misfortunes! Now I pray thee, O Mother Devi, that thou wilt be my helper also, and fulfil the desire of my heart. And if by thy favor I be enabled to marry that loveliest of women, O Devi, verily I will make a sacrifice of my own head to thee." Such was the vow which he vowed.

But having returned unto his city and to his home, the torment of being separated from his beloved so wrought upon him that he became grievously sick, knowing neither sleep nor hunger nor thirst, inasmuch as love causes men to forget all these things. And it seemed that he might shortly die. Then, indeed, his friend, being alarmed, went to the father of the youth, and told him all, so that the father also became fearful for his son. Therefore, accompanied by his son's friend, he went to that city, and sought out the father of the girl, and said to him : "Lo! I am of thy caste and calling, and I have a favor to ask of thee. It has come to pass that my son is so enamored of thy daughter that unless she be wedded to him he will surely die. Give me, therefore, the hand of thy daughter for my dear son." And the other was not at all displeased at these words ; but, sending for a Brahman, he decided upon a day of good omen for the marriage to be celebrated. And he said : "Friend, bring thy son hither. I shall rub her hands with turmeric, that all men may know she is betrothed."

Thus was the marriage arranged ; and in due time the father of the youth came with his son to the city ; and after the ceremony had been fulfilled, he returned to his own people with his son and his daughter-in-law. Now the love these young people held each for the other waxed greater day by day; and there was no shadow on the young man's happiness saving the memory of his vow. But his wife so caressed and fondled him that at last the recollection of the oath faded utterly away.

After many days it happened that the husband and wife were both invited to a feast at Dharmpur; and they went thither with the friend who had before accompanied the youth upon his pilgrimage. Even as they neared the city, they saw from afar off the peaked and gilded summits of Devi's temple. Then the remembrance of his oath came back with great anguish to that young husband. "Verily," he thought within his heart, "I am most shameless and wicked among all perjurers, having been false in my vow even to Devi, Mother of Gods!"

And he said to his friend: "I pray thee, remain thou here with my wife while I go to prostrate myself before Devi." So he departed to the temple, and bathed himself in the sacred pool, and bowed himself before the statue with joined hands. And having performed the rites ordained, he struck himself with a sword a mighty blow upon his neck, so that his head, being separated from his body, rolled even to the pillared stem of the marble lotos upon which Devi sat.

Now after the wife and the dead man's friend had long waited vainly, the friend said: " Surely he hath been gone a great time ; remain thou here while I go to bring him back ! " So he went to the temple, and entering it beheld his friend's body lying in blood, and the severed head beneath the feet of Devi. And he said to his own heart: " Verily this world is hard to live in ! . . . Should I now return, the people would say that I had murdered this man for the sake of his wife's exceeding beauty." Therefore he likewise bathed in the sacred pool, and performed the rites prescribed, and smote himself upon the neck so that his head also was severed from his body and rolled in like manner unto Devi's feet.

Now, after the young wife had waited in vain alone for a long while, she became much tormented by fear for her husband's sake, and went also to the temple. And when she beheld the corpses and the reeking swords, she wept with unspeakable anguish, and said to her own heart: " Surely this world is hard to live in at best ; and what is life now worth to me without my husband? Moreover, people will say that I, being a wicked woman, murdered them both, in order to live wickedly without restraint. Let me therefore also make a sacrifice!"...

Saying these words, she departed to the sacred pool and bathed therein, and, having performed the holy rites, lifted a sword to her own smooth throat that she might slay herself. But even as she lifted the sword a mighty hand of marble stayed her arm; while the deep pavement quivered to the tread of Devi's feet. For the Mother of Gods had arisen, and descended from her lotos seat, and stood beside her. And a divine voice issued from the grim lips of stone, saying, "O daughter! dear hast thou made thyself to me! ask now a boon of Devi!" But she answered, all-tremblingly, "Divinest Mother, I pray only that these men may be restored to life." Then said the goddess, "Put their heads upon their bodies."

And the beautiful wife sought to do according to the divine command; but love and hope and the fear of Devi made dizzy her brain, so that she placed her husband's head upon the friend's neck, and the head of the friend upon the neck of her husband. And the goddess sprinkled the bodies with the nectar of immortality, and they stood up, alive and well, indeed, yet with heads wonderfully exchanged.

.*.

Then said the Demon: " O King Vikramaditya! to which of
these two was she wife?   Verily, if thou dost not rightly answer,
I shall devour thee."   And Vikramaditya answered: " Listen!
in the holy Shastra it is said that as the Ganges is chief among
rivers, and Sumeru chief among mountains, and the Tree of
Paradise chief among trees, so is the head chief among the parts
of the body.   Therefore she was the wife of that one to whose
body her husband's head was joined.". . . Having answered
rightly, the king suffered no hurt; but inasmuch as he had
spoken, it was permitted the corpse-demon to return to the tree,
and hang suspended therefrom above the tombs.

. . . And many times, in like manner, was the Demon enabled
to return to the tree; and even so many times did Vikramaditya
take down and bind and bear away the Demon; and each time
the Demon would relate to the king a story so wild, so wonderful,
that he could not choose but hear. . . . Now this is another of those
tales which the Demon told: —

O king, in the city of Dharmasthal there lived
a Brahman, called Kesav; and his daughter, who
was beautiful as an Apsara, had rightly been
named Sweet Jasmine-Flower, Madhumalati. And
so soon as she was nubile, her father and her
mother and her brothers were all greatly anxious
to find her a worthy husband.

Now one day the father and the brother and
the mother of the girl each promised her hand
to a different suitor.   For the good Kesav, while
absent upon a holy visit, met a certain Brahman
youth, who so pleased him that Kesav promised

him Madhumalati; and even the same day, the brother, who was a student of the Shastras, met at the house of his spiritual teacher another student who so pleased him that he promised him Madhumalati; and in the mean time there visited Kesav's home another young Brahman, who so delighted the mother that she promised him Madhumalati. And the three youths thus betrothed to the girl were all equal in beauty, in strength, in accomplishments, and even in years, so that it would not have been possible to have preferred any one of them above the rest. Thus, when the father returned home, he found the three youths there before him; and he was greatly troubled upon learning all that had taken place. "Verily," he exclaimed, "there is but one girl and three bridegrooms, and to all of the three has our word been pledged; to whom shall I give Madhumalati?" And he knew not what to do.

But even as he was thinking, and gazing from one to the other of the three youths, a hooded serpent bit the girl, so that she died.

Forthwith the father sent out for magicians and holy men, that they might give back life to his daughter; and the holy men came together with the magicians. But the enchanters said that, by reason of the period of the moon, it was not possible for them to do aught; and the holy men avowed that even Brahma himself could not restore life to one bitten by a serpent. With sore lamentation, accordingly, the Brahman performed the funeral rites; and a pyre was built, and the body of Madhumalati consumed thereupon.

Now those three youths had beheld the girl in her living beauty, and all of them had been madly enamoured of her; and each one, because he had loved and lost her, resolved thenceforth to abandon the world and forego all pleasure in this life. All visited the funeral pyre; and one of them gathered up all the girl's bones while they were yet warm from the flame, and tied them within a bag, and then went his way to become a fakir. Another collected the ashes of her body, and took them with him into the recesses of a forest, where he built a hut and began to live alone with the memory of her. The last indeed took no relic of Madhumalati, but, having prayed a prayer, assumed the garb of a Yogi, and departed to beg his way through the world. Now his name was Madhusudam.

Long after these things had happened, Madhusudam one day entered the house of a Brahman, to beg for alms; and the Brahman invited him to partake of the family repast. So Madhusudam, having washed his hands and his feet, sate him down to eat beside the Brahman; and the Brahman's wife waited upon them. Now it came to pass, when the meal was still but half served, that the Brahman's little boy asked for food; and being bidden to wait, he clung to the skirt of his mother's dress, so that she was hindered in her duties of hospitality. Becoming angry, therefore, she seized her boy, and threw him into the fire-place where a great fire was; and the boy was burned to ashes in a moment. But the Brahman continued to eat as if nothing had happened; and his wife continued to serve the repast with a kindly smile upon her countenance.

And being horror-stricken at these sights, Mad-husudam arose from his sitting-place, leaving his meal unfinished, and directed his way toward the door. Then the Brahman kindly questioned him, saying: " O friend, how comes it that thou dost not eat? Surely both I and my wife have done what we could to please thee! "

And Madhusudam, astonished and wroth, an-swered: " How dost thou dare ask me why I do not eat? how might any being, excepting a Rak-shasa, eat in the house of one by whom such a demon-deed hath been committed? " But the Brahman smiled, and rose up and went to another part of the house, and returned speedily with a book of incantations, — a book of the science of resurrection. And he read but one incantation therefrom, when, lo! the boy that had been burned came alive and unscorched from the fire, and ran to his mother, crying and clinging to her dress as before.

Then Madhusudam thought within himself: "Had I that wondrous book, how readily might I restore my beloved to life!" And he sat down again, and, having finished his repast, remained in that house as a guest. But in the middle of the night he arose stealthily, and purloined the magical book, and fled away to his own city.

And after many days he went upon a pilgrimage of love to the place where the body of Madhumalati had been burned (for it was the anniversary of her death), and arriving he found that the other two who had been betrothed to her were also there before him. And lifting up their voices, they cried out: "O Madhusudam! thou hast been gone many years and hast seen much. What hast thou learned of science?"

But he answered: "I have learned the science that restores the dead to life." Then they prayed him, saying, "Revive thou Madhumalati!' And he told them: "Gather ye her bones together, and her ashes, and I will give her life."

And they having so done, Madhusudam produced the book and read a charm therefrom ; and the heap of ashes and cindered bones shaped itself to the command, and changed color, and lived, and became a beautiful woman, sweet as a jasmine-flower, — Madhumalati even as she was before the snake had bitten her!

But the three youths, beholding her smile, were blinded by love, so that they began to wrangle fiercely together for the sake of her. . . .

Then the Demon said: " O Vikramaditaya! to which of these was she wife? Answer rightly, lest I devour thee."

And the king answered: " Truly she was the wife of him who had collected her ashes, and taken them with him into the recesses of the forest, where he built a hut and dwelt alone with the memory of her."

" Nay!" said the Demon, " how could she have been restored to life had not the other also preserved her bones? and despite the piety of those two, how could she have been resurrected but for the third?"

But the king replied: " Even as the son's duty is to preserve the bones of his parents, so did he who preserved the bones of Madhumalati stand to her only in the place of a son. Even as a father giveth life, so did he who reanimated Madhumalati stand to her only in the place of a father. But he who collected her ashes and took them with him into the recesses of the forest, where

7

he built a hut and dwelt alone with the memory of her, he was
truly her lover and rightful husband."

⁎⁎

. . . Many other hard questions the Demon also asked, concern-
ing men who by magic turned themselves into women, and con-
cerning corpses animated by evil spirits; but the king answered
all of them save one, which indeed admitted of no answer : —

O Vikramaditaya, when Mahabal was rajah of
Dharmpur, another monarch strove against him,
and destroyed his army in a great battle, and
slew him. And the wife and daughter of the
dead king fled to the forest for safety, and wandered there alone. At that time the rajah Chandrasen was hunting in the forest, and his son
with him ; and they beheld the prints of women's
feet upon the ground. Then said Chandrasen :
" Surely the feet of those who have passed here
are delicate and beautiful, like those of women ;
yet I marvel exceedingly that there should be
women in this desolate place. Let us pursue
after them ; and if they be beautiful, I shall take
to wife her whose feet have made the smallest
of these tracks, and thou shalt wed the other."
So they came up with the women, and were
much charmed with their beauty ; and the rajah
Chandrasen married the daughter of the dead
Mahabel, and Chandrasen's son took Mahabel's

widow to wife. So that the father married the daughter of the mother, and the son the mother of the daughter. . . .

And the Demon asked: " O Vikramaditaya, in what manner were the children of Chandrasen and his son related by these marriages? " But the king could not answer. And because he remained silent the Demon was pleased, and befriended him in a strange and unexpected manner, as it is written in the VETÁLA-PANTCHAVINSATI.

———◆———

THE LION.

Intelligence is better than much learning; intelligence is better than science; the man that hath not intelligence shall perish like those who made unto themselves a lion. . . . And this is the story of the lion, as related by the holy Brahman Vichnousarman in the PANTCHOPAKHYANA.

IN days of old there were four youths of the Brahman caste, — brothers, who loved each other with strong affection, and had resolved to travel all together into a neighboring empire to seek fortune and fame.

Of these four brothers three had deeply studied all sciences, knowing magic, astronomy, alchemy, and occult arts most difficult to learn; while the fourth had no knowledge whatever of science, possessing intelligence only.

Now, as they were travelling together, one of the learned brothers observed: "Why should a brother without knowledge obtain profit by our wisdom? Travelling with us he can be only a burden upon us. Never will he be able to obtain the respect of kings, and therefore must he remain a disgrace to us. Rather let him return home."

But the eldest of all answered: "Nay! let him share our good luck; for he is our loving brother, and we may perhaps find some position for him which he can fill without being a disgrace to us."

So they journeyed along; and after a time, while passing through a forest, they beheld the bones of a lion scattered on the path. These bones were white as milk and hard as flint, so dry and so bleached they were.

Then said he who had first condemned the ignorance of his brother: "Let us now show our brother what science may accomplish; let us put his ignorance to shame by giving life to these lion-bones, and creating another lion from them! By a few magical words I can summon the dry bones together, making each fit into its place." Therewith he spake the words, so that the dry bones came together with a clattering sound, —

each fitting to its socket, — and the skeleton re-jointed itself together.

"I," quoth the second brother, "can by a few words spread tendons over the bones, — each in its first place, — and thicken them with muscle, and redden them with blood, and create the humors, the veins, the glands, the marrow, the internal organs, and the exterior skin." Therewith he spake the words; and the body of the lion appeared upon the ground at their feet, perfect, shaggy, huge.

"And I," said the third brother, "can by one word give warmth to the blood and motion to the heart, so that the animal shall live and breathe and devour beasts. And ye shall hear him roar."

But ere he could utter the word, the fourth brother, who knew nothing about science, placed his hand over his mouth. "Nay!" he cried, "do not utter the word. That is a lion! If thou givest him life, he will devour us."

But the others laughed him to scorn, saying: "Go home, thou fool! what dost thou know of science?"

Then he answered them: "At least, delay the making of the lion until thy brother can climb up this tree." Which they did.

But hardly had he ascended the tree when the

word was spoken, and the lion moved and opened his great yellow eyes. Then he stretched himself, and arose, and roared. Then he turned upon the three wise men, and slew them, and devoured them.

But after the lion had departed, the youth who knew nothing of science descended from the tree unharmed, and returned to his home.

———◆———

THE LEGEND OF THE MONSTER MISFORTUNE.

He that hath a hundred desireth a thousand; he that hath a thousand would have a hundred thousand; he that hath a hundred thousand longeth for the kingdom; he that hath a kingdom doth wish to possess the heavens. And being led astray by cupidity, even the owners of riches and wisdom do those things which should never be done, and seek after that which ought never to be sought after. . . . Wherefore there hath been written, for the benefit of those who do nourish their own evil passions, this legend taken from the forty-sixth book of the FA-YOUEN-TCHOU-LIN.

In those ages when the sun shone brighter than in these years, when the perfumes of flowers were sweeter, when the colors of the world were fairer to behold, and gods were wont to walk upon earth, there was a certain happy kingdom wherein no misery was. Of gems and of gold there was superabundance; the harvests were inexhaustible as ocean; the cities more populous than ant-hills. So many years had passed without war that plants grew upon the walls of the great towns, disjointing the rampart-stones by the snaky strength of their roots. And through all that land there was a murmur of music constant as the flow of the Yellow River; sleep alone interrupted the pursuit of pleasure, and even the dreams of sleepers were never darkened by imaginary woe. For there was no sickness and no want of any sort, so that each man lived his century of years, and dying laid him down painlessly, as one seeking repose after pleasure, — the calm of slumber after the intoxication of joy.

***

One day the king of that country called all his counsellors and ministers and chief mandarins together, and questioned them, saying: "Behold! I have read in certain ancient annals which are kept within our chief temple, these words: '*In days of old Misfortune visited the land.*' Is there among you one who can tell me what manner of creature Misfortune is? Unto what may Misfortune be likened?"

But all the counsellors and the ministers and the mandarins answered: " O king, we have never beheld it, nor can we say what manner of creature it may be."

Thereupon the king ordered one of his ministers to visit all the lesser kingdoms, and to inquire what manner of creature Misfortune might be, and to purchase it at any price, — if indeed it could be bought, — though the price should be the value of a province.

Now there was a certain god, who, seeing and hearing these things, forthwith assumed the figure of a man, and went to the greatest market of a neighboring kingdom, taking with him Misfortune, chained with a chain of iron. And the form of Misfortune was the form of a gigantic sow. So the minister, visiting that foreign market, observed the creature, which was made fast to a pillar there, and asked the god what animal it was.

" It is called the female of Misfortune," quoth the god.

" Is it for sale?" questioned the minister.

" Assuredly," answered the god.

" And the price?"

" A million pieces of gold."

" What is its daily food?"

" One bushel measure of needles."

⁂

Having paid for the beast a million pieces of good yellow gold, the minister was perforce compelled to procure food for it. So he sent out runners to all the markets, and to the shops of tailors and of weavers, and to all the mandarins of all districts within the kingdom, to procure needles. This caused much tribulation in the land, not only by reason of the scarcity of needles, but also because of the affliction to which the people were subjected. For those who had not needles were beaten with bamboos; and the mandarins, desiring to obey the behest of the king's minister, exercised much severity. The tailors and others who lived by their needles soon found themselves in a miserable plight; and the needlemakers, toil as they would, could never make enough to satisfy the hunger of the beast, although many died because of overwork. And the price of a needle became as the price of emeralds and diamonds, and the rich gave all their substance to procure food for this beast, whose mouth, like the mouth of hell, could not be satisfied. Then the people in many parts, made desperate by hunger and the severity of the mandarins, rose in revolt, provoking a war which caused the destruction of many tens of thousands. The rivers ran with blood, yet the minister could not bring the beast to the palace for lack of needles wherewith to feed it.

Therefore he wrote at last to the king, saying: " I have indeed been able to find and to buy the female of Misfortune; but the male I have not been able to obtain, nor, with your Majesty's permission, will I seek for it. Lo! the female hath already devoured the substance of this land; and I dare not attempt to bring such a monster to the palace. I pray your Majesty therefore that your Majesty graciously accord me leave to destroy this hideous beast; and I trust that your Majesty will bear in mind the saying of the wise men of India: ' *Even a King who will not hearken to advice should be advised by faithful counsellors.*' "

Then the king, being already alarmed by noise of the famine and of the revolution, ordered that the beast should be destroyed.

***

Accordingly, the female of Misfortune was led to a desolate place without the village, and chained fast with chains of iron; and the minister commanded the butchers to kill it. But so impenetrable was its skin that neither axe nor knife could wound it. Wherefore the soldiers were commanded to destroy it. But the arrows of the archers flattened their steel points upon Misfortune, even when directed against its eyes, which were bright and hard as diamonds; while swords and spears innumerable were shattered and broken in foolish efforts to kill it.

Then the minister commanded a great fire to be built; and the monster was bound within the fire, while quantities of pitch and of oil and of resinous woods were poured and piled upon the flame, until the fire became too hot for men to approach it within the distance of ten *li*. But the beast, instead of burning, first became red hot and then white hot, shining like the moon. Its chains melted like wax, so that it escaped at last and ran out among the people like a dragon of fire. Many were thus consumed; and the beast entered the villages and destroyed them; and still running so swiftly that its heat increased with its course, it entered the capital city, and ran through it and over it upon the roofs, burning up even the king in his palace.

Thus, by the folly of that king, was the kingdom utterly wasted and destroyed, so that it became a desert, inhabited only by lizards and serpents and demons. . . .

NOTE. — This and the following fable belong to the curious collection translated by M. Stanislas Julien from

a Chinese encyclopædia, and published at Paris in 1860, un‑
der the title, "Les Avadânas," — or "The Similitudes," —
a Sanscrit term corresponding to the Chinese *Pi-yu*, and
justified by the origin of the stories, translated by the Chi‑
nese themselves, or at least reconstructed, from old Sanscrit
texts.   I have ventured, however, to accentuate the slightly
Chinese coloring of the above grotesque parable. — L. H.

A PARABLE BUDDHISTIC.

*. . . Like to earthen vessels wrought in a potter's mill, so are the
lives of men; howsoever carefully formed, all are doomed to de‑
struction.   Nought that exists shall endure ; life is as the waters
of a river that flow away, but never return.   Therefore may hap‑
piness only be obtained by concealing the Six Appetites, as the
tortoise withdraws its six extremities into its shell; by guarding
the thoughts from desire and from grief, even as the city is
guarded by its ditches and its walls. . . .*

So spoke in gathas Sakya-Mouni.   And this
parable, doubtless by him narrated of old, and
translated from a lost Indian manuscript into the
Chinese tongue, may be found in the fifty-first
book of the " Fa-youen-tchou-lin."

. . . A father and his son were laboring to‑
gether in the field during the season of serpents,
and a hooded serpent bit the young man, so that

he presently died. For there is no remedy known to man which may annul the venom of the hooded snake, filling the eyes with sudden darkness and stilling the motion of the heart. But the father, seeing his son lying dead, and the ants commencing to gather, returned to his work and ceased not placidly to labor as before.

Then a Brahman passing that way, seeing what had happened, wondered that the father continued to toil, and yet more at observing that his eyes were tearless. Therefore he questioned him, asking: "Whose son was that youth who is dead?"

"He was mine own son," returned the laborer, ceasing not to labor.

"Yet, being thy son, how do I find thee tearless and impassive?"

"Folly!" answered the laborer; — "even the instant that a man is born into the world, so soon doth he make his first step in the direction of death; and the ripeness of his strength is also the beginning of its decline. For the well-doing there is indeed a recompense; for the wicked there is likewise punishment. What avail, therefore, tears and grief? in no wise can they serve the dead. . . . Perchance, good Brahman, thou art on thy way to the city. If so, I pray thee to pass by my house, and to tell my wife that my son is dead, so that she may send hither my noonday repast."

"Ah! what manner of man is this?" thought the Brahman to himself. "His son is dead, yet he does not weep; the corpse lies under the sun, yet he ceases not to labor; the ants gather about it, yet he coldly demands his noonday meal! Surely there is no compassion, no human feeling, within his entrails!" These things the Brahman thought to himself; yet, being stirred by curiosity, he proceeded none the less to the house of the laborer, and beholding the mother said unto her: "Woman, thy son is dead, having been stricken by a hooded snake; and thy tearless husband bade me tell thee to send him his noonday repast. . . . And now I perceive thou art also insensible to the death of thy son, for thou dost not weep!"

But the mother of the dead answered him with comparisons, saying: "Sir, that son had indeed received only a passing life from his parents; therefore I called him not my son. Now he hath passed away from me, nor was it in my feeble power to retain him. He was only as a traveller halting at a tavern; the traveller rests and passes on; shall the tavern keeper restrain him? Such is indeed the relation of mother and son. Whether the son go or come, whether he remain or pass on, I have no power over his being ; my son has fulfilled the destiny appointed, and from that destiny none could save him. Why, therefore, lament that which is inevitable ? "

And wondering still more, the Brahman turned unto the eldest sister of the dead youth, a maiden in the lotos bloom of her maidenhood, and asked her, saying : " Thy brother is dead, and wilt thou not weep ? "

But the maiden also answered him with comparisons, saying : " Sometimes a strong woodman enters the forest of trees, and hews them down with mighty axe-strokes, and binds them together into a great raft, and launches the raft into the vast river. But a furious wind arises and excites the waves to dash the raft hither and thither, so that it breaks asunder, and the currents separate the foremost logs from those behind, and all are whirled away never again to be united. Even such has been the fate of my young brother. We were bound together by destiny in the one family ; we have been separated forever. There is no fixed time of life or death ; whether our existence be long or short, we are united only for a period, to be separated forevermore. My brother has ended his allotted career; each of us is following a destiny that may not be changed. To me it was not given to protect and to save him. Wherefore should I weep for that which could not be prevented?"

Then wondering still more, the Brahman addressed himself to the beautiful wife of the dead youth, saying: "And thou, on whose bosom he slept, dost thou not weep for him, thy comely husband, cut off in the summer of his manhood?"

But she answered him also with comparisons, saying: "Even as two birds, flying one from the east and one from the south, meet and look into each other's eyes, and circle about each other, and seek the same summit of tree or temple, and sleep together until the dawn, so was our own fate. When the golden light breaks in the east, the two birds, leaving their temple perch or their tree, fly in opposite ways each to seek its food. They meet again if destiny wills; if not, they never behold each other more. Such was the fate of my husband and myself; when death sought him his destiny was accomplished, and it was not in my power to save him. Therefore, why should I weep?"

Then wondering more than ever, the Brahman

questioned the slave of the dead man, asking him: " Thy master is dead ; why dost thou not weep?"

But the slave also answered him with comparisons, saying: " My master and I were united by the will of destiny ; I was only as the little calf which follows the great bull. The great bull is slain : the little calf could not save him from the axe of the butcher ; its cries and bleatings could avail nothing. Wherefore should I weep, not knowing how soon indeed my own hour may come?"

And the Brahman, silent with wonder, watched the slender figures of the women moving swiftly to and fro athwart the glow of golden light from without, preparing the noonday repast for the tearless laborer in the field.

PUNDARI.

A story of the Buddha, who filled with light the world, the soles of whose feet were like unto the faces of two blazing suns, for that he trod in the Perfect Paths.

. . . In those days Buddha was residing upon the summit of the mountain Gridhrakuta, over-

looking that ancient and vanished city called
Rajagriha, — then a glorious vision of white
streets and fretted arcades, and milky palaces
so mightily carven that they seemed light as
woofs of Cashmere, delicate as frost! There
was the cry of elephants heard; there the air
quivered with amorous music; there the flowers
of a thousand gardens exhaled incense to heaven,
and there women sweeter than the flowers moved
their braceleted ankles to the notes of harps and
flutes. . . . But, above all, the summit of the mountain glowed with a glory greater than day, — with
a vast and rosy light signalling the presence of
the Buddha.

Now in that city dwelt a bayadere, most lovely
among women, with whom in grace no other being could compare; and she had become weary
of the dance and the jewels and the flowers, —
weary of her corselets of crimson and golden silk,
and her robes light as air, diaphanous as mist,
— weary, also, of the princes who rode to her
dwelling upon elephants, bearing her gifts of jewels and perfumes and vessels strangely wrought
in countries distant ten years' journey. And her
heart whispered her to seek out Buddha, that she
might obtain knowledge and rest, becoming even
as a Bikshuni.

Therefore, bidding farewell to the beautiful city, she began to ascend the hilly paths to where the great and rosy glory beamed above. Fierce was the heat of the sun, and rough the dizzy paths ; and the thirst and weariness of deserts came upon her. So that, having but half ascended the mountain, she paused to drink and rest at a spring clear and bright like diamond, that had wrought a wondrous basin for itself in the heart of the rock.

But as the bayadere bent above the fountain to drink, she beheld in its silver-bright mirror the black glory of her hair, and the lotos softness of her silky-shadowed eyes, and the rose-budding of her honey-sweet mouth, and her complexion golden as sunlight, and the polished suppleness of her waist, and her slender limbs rounder than an elephant's trunk, and the gold-engirdled grace of her ankles. And a mist of tears gathered before her sight. " Shall I, indeed, cast away this beauty? " she murmured. " Shall I mask this loveliness, that hath allured rajahs and maharajahs, beneath the coarse garb of a recluse? Shall I behold my youth and grace fade away in solitude as dreams of the past? Wherefore, then, should I have been born so beautiful? Nay! let those without grace and without youth abandon all to seek the Five Paths ! " And she turned her face again toward the white-glimmering Rajagriha, whence ascended the breath of flowers, and the liquid melody of flutes, and the wanton laughter of dancing girls. . . .

But far above, in the rosiness, omniscient Buddha looked into her heart, and, pitying her weakness, changed himself by utterance of the Word into a girl far comelier and yet more lissome than even Pundari the bayadere. So that Pundari, descending, suddenly and in much astonishment became aware of the loveliest of companions at her side, and asked: "O thou fairest one! whence comest thou? Who may the kindred be of one so lovely?"

And the sweet stranger answered, in tones softer than of flutes of gold: "I also, lovely one, am returning to the white city Rajagriha; let us journey together, that we may comfort each other by the way."

And Pundari answered: "Yea, O fairest maiden! thy beauty draws me to thee as the flower the bee, and thy heart must surely be precious as is thy incomparable face!"

So they journeyed on; but the lovely stranger became weary at last, and Pundari, sitting down, made a pillow of her round knees for the dainty head, and kissed her comrade to sleep, and stroked the silky magnificence of her hair, and fondled the ripe beauty of the golden face slumbering, and a great love for the stranger swelled ripening in her heart.

Yet while she gazed the face upon her smooth knees changed, even as a golden fruit withers and wrinkles, so wizened became the curved cheeks: strange hollows darkened and deepened about the eyes; the silky lashes vanished with their shadows; the splendid hair whitened like the ashes of altar fires; shrunken and shrivelled grew the lips; toothless yawned the once rosy mouth; and the bones of the face, made salient, fore-shaped the gibbering outlines of a skull. The perfume of youth was gone; but there arose odors insufferable of death, and with them came the ghastly creeping things that death fattens, and the livid colors and blotches that his shadowy fingers leave. And Pundari, shrieking, fled to the presence of Buddha, and related unto him the things which she had seen.

And the World-honored comforted her, and spake: —

"O Pundari, life is but as the fruit; loveliness but as the flower! Of what use is the fairest body that lieth rotting beside the flowings of the Ganges? Old age and death none of us may

escape ; yet there are worse than these, — the
new births which are to this life as the echo to
the voice in the cavern, as the great footprints
to the steps of the elephant.

" From desire cometh woe ; by desire is begotten all evil. The body itself is a creation of the
mind only, of the foolish thirst of the heart for
pleasure. As the shadows of dreams are dissipated with the awakening of the sleeper, even
so shall sorrow vanish and evil pass away from
the heart of whosoever shall learn to conquer desire and quench the heart's thirst ; even so shall
the body itself vanish for those who tread well in
the Five Paths.

" O Pundari, there is no burning greater than
desire ; no joy like unto the destruction of the
body ! Even as the white stork standing alone
beside the dried-up lily-pool, so shall those be
whose youth passes from them in the fierce heat
of foolish passion ; and when the great change
shall come, they will surely be born again unto
foolishness and tears.

" Those only who have found delight in the
wilderness where others behold horror ; those
who have extinguished all longings ; those self-
made passionless by meditation on life and death,
— only such do attain to happiness, and, prevent-

ing the second birth, enter into the blessedness of Nirvana.". . .

And the bayadère, cutting off her hair, and casting from her all gifts of trinkets and jewels, abandoned everything to enter the Five Paths. And the Devas, rejoicing, made radiant the mountains above the white city, and filled the air with a rain of strange flowers. And whosoever would know more of Buddha, let him read the marvellous book "Fah-Kheu-King," — the Book "Dhammapada."

————◆————

YAMARAJA.

The Legend Maggavago; or, " The Way," — which is in the marvellous book of the Dhammapada. . . . *A story of the Buddha at whose birth the stars stopped in their courses.* . . .

THE Brahman's son was dead, — dead in the blossoming of his beautiful youth, as the rose in whose heart a worm is born, as the lotos bud when the waters of the pool are cut off. (For comeliness there was none like him, even among the children of the holiest caste; nor were there any so deeply learned in the books of religion, in just reasoning regarding the Scriptures, in the

recitation of the slokas of singers divinely inspired. Thrice the aged priest fainted away
upon the body of his son; and as often as they
would have led him to his home, he shrieked and
fainted again, so that, at last, even while he lay
as dead, they took the body from his arms, and,
having washed it with the waters of purification,
wrapped it in perfumed linen, and laid it upon
a bier decked with Indian flowers, and bore it
away to the place of interment. Thus, when the
unhappy father came to himself, all was accomplished; and the stern elders of his caste, gathering
about him, so harshly reproved him for his grief
that he was perforce compelled to reason with
himself regarding the vanity of lamentation and
the folly of human tears.

* *
*

But not ceasing to meditate upon his great loss,
a wild hope at last shaped itself within his heart.
"Lo!" he thought, "I have heard it said that certain mighty Brahmans, having acquired the Five
Virtues, the Five Faculties, the Ten Forces, were
enabled to converse face to face with Yamaraja,
the Lord of Death! To me it hath not indeed
been given, by reason perchance of my feeble
will, to obtain the supreme wisdom; yet my love
and faith are of the heart, and I will seek out

Yamaraja, King of Death, and pray him to give
me back my son." Therefore the Brahman, investing himself with sacerdotal vestments, performed the holy ceremonies ordained in the law;
and having offered the sacrifice of flowers and of
incense, he departed to seek the Lord of Death,
the Maharajah of vanished kingdoms, Yama.
And he questioned all whom he met as to where
Yama might be found.

* *
*

Some, opening astounded eyes, answered him
not at all, deeming him to be mad; some there
were that mocked him; some counselled that he
should return home, lest he find Yama too speedily! Kshatrya princes with jewel-hilted sabres
answered him as they rode by in glittering steel
and glimmering gold: "Yama may be found in
the tempest of battles, beneath the bursting of
arrow-clouds, amidst the lightning of swords, before the armored ranks of the fighting elephants."
Swarthy mariners replied, with rough laughter as
of sea winds: "Thou mayst seek Yama in the
roaring of waters and raving of typhoons; let the
spirit of storms answer thee!" . . . And dancing girls, singing the burning hymn of Ourvasi,
paused to answer with their witchery: "Seek
Yama rather in our arms, upon our lips, upon

our hearts; exhale thy soul in a kiss." ...
And they laughed shrilly as the bells of the
temple caves laugh when the wind lips their
silver tongues.

***

So he wandered on, by the banks of many
rivers, under the shadowing of many city walls,
still seeking, until he came to the great wilderness
below the mountains of the east, where dwelt the
most holy, who had obtained supreme wisdom.
Serpents hooded like mendicants protruded their
forked tongues; the leopard thrust aside the jungle grasses to gaze at him with eyes of green
flame; the boa moved before him, making a
waving in the deep weeds as the wake of a boat
upon water. But inasmuch as he sought Yama,
he could not fear.

Thus he came at last to where the most holy of
Brahmans dwelt, who had obtained supreme wisdom, nourishing themselves upon the perfumes
of flowers only. The shadow of the rocks, the
shadows of the primeval trees, lengthened and
shortened and circled with the circling of the
sun; but the shadows of the trees beneath which
they sat circled not, nor did they change with
the changing of the universal light. The eyes
of the hermits gazed unwinking upon the face

of the sun; the birds of heaven nestled in the
immobility of their vast beards. All tremblingly he asked of them where Yamaraja might
be found.

***

Long he awaited in silence their answer,
hearing only the waters chanting their eternal
slokas, the trees whispering with all their flickering leaf-tongues, the humming of innumerable
golden flies, the heavy movement of great beasts
in the jungle. At last the Brahmans moved their
lips, and answered, "Wherefore seekest thou
Yama?" And at their utterance the voices of
the waters and the woods were hushed; the
golden flies ceased the music of their wings.

Then answered the pilgrim, tremblingly: "Lo!
I also am a Brahman, ye holy ones; but to me it
hath not been given to obtain the supreme wisdom, seeing that I am unworthy to know the
Absolute. Yet I sought diligently for the space
of sixty years to obtain holiness; and our law
teaches that if one have not reached wisdom at
sixty, it is his duty, returning home, to take a
wife, that he may have holy children. This I did;
and one son was born unto me, beautiful as the
Vassika flower, learned even in his childhood.
And I did all I could to instil into him the love

of uttermost wisdom, teaching him myself until
it came to pass that he knew more than I, wherefore I sought him teachers from Elephanta. And
in the beauty of his youth he was taken from me,
— borne away with the silk of manhood already
shadowing his lip. Wherefore I pray ye, holy
men, tell me in what place Yamaraja dwells, that
I may pray him to give me back my boy!"

***

Then all the holy voices answered together as
one voice, as the tone of many waters flowing in
one cadence; " Verily thou hast not been fitted
to seek the supreme wisdom, seeing that in the
winter of thine age thou dost still mourn by
reason of a delusion. For the stars die in their
courses, the heavens wither as leaves, the worlds
vanish as the smoke of incense. Lives are as
flower-petals opening to fade; the works of
man as verses written upon water. (He who
hath reached supreme wisdom mourneth existence only. . . . Yet, that thou mayst be enlight-
ened, we will even advise thee.) The kingdom
of Yama thou mayst not visit, for no man may
tread the way with mortal feet. But many hundred leagues toward the setting of the sun, there
is a valley, with a city shining in the midst
thereof. There no man dwells, but the gods

only, when they incarnate themselves to live upon
earth. And upon the eighth day of each month
Yamaraja visits them, and thou mayst see him.
(Yet beware of failing a moment to practise the
ceremonies, to recite the Mantras, lest a strange
evil befall thee !) . . Depart now from us, that we
may re-enter into contemplation ! "

*
* *

So, after journeying many moons, the good
Brahman stood at last upon the height above the
valley, and saw the ivory-white city — a vision
of light, like the heaven Trayastrinshas. Not
Hanoumat, the messenger of Rama, beheld such
splendor, when he haunted the courts of Lanka
by night, and beheld in Ravana's palace the loveliest of women interlaced in the embrace of sleep,
" the garland of women's bodies interwoven."
Terraces fretted by magical chisels rose heaven-
ward, tier upon tier, until their summit seemed
but the fleeciness of summer clouds ; arches tow-
ered upon arches ; pink marble gates yawned like
the mouths of slumbering bayaderes ; crenellated
walls edged with embroidery of inlaid gold surrounded gardens deep as forests ; domes white-
rounded, like breasts, made pearly curves against
the blue ; fountains, silver-nippled, showered perfumed spray ; and above the great gate of the

palace of the gods, where Devas folded their
wings on guard, flamed a vast carbuncle, upon
whose face was graven the Word comprehended
only by those who have attained supreme wisdom.
And standing before the gate, the Brahman burnt
the holy incense and recited the holy Mantras, . . .
until the Devas, pitying him, rolled back the doors
of gold, and bade him enter.

* *

Lofty as heaven seemed that palace hall, whose
vault of cerulean blue hung, self-sustained, above
the assembly of the gods; and the pavement of
sable marble glimmered like a fathomless lake.
Yet, as the Brahman prostrated himself, not daring
to lift his eyes, he felt that it quavered under the
tread of mortal feet even as when earth trembles.
In its reflection he beheld the gods seated in assembly, not awful of image as in earthly temples,
but as beings of light, star-diademed, rosy with
immortality. . . . Only Yamaraja's brow bore no
starry flame; and there was in his gaze a pro-
fundity as of deep answering unto deep. To the
ears of the worshipper his voice came like the
voice of waters pouring over the verge of an echo-
less abyss, . . . and in obedience to that voice the
Brahman uttered his prayer.

And the Lord of Death, replying in strange

tones, said : " Pious and just is this prayer, O
child of Brahma ! Thy son is now in the Garden
of the East. Take him by the hand and go thy
way."...

* * *

Joyfully the Brahman entered that garden of
fountains that flow forever ; of fruits, eternally
ripe, that never fall ; of flowers immortal, that
never fade. And he discerned, among children
innumerable disporting, his own beloved son play-
ing beside the fountains ; so that he cried out with
a great cry, and ran to him and clasped him and
wept over him, exclaiming : " O sweet son ! O my
beloved first-born ! dost thou not know me, thy
father who mourned thee so long, — who hath even
entered the presence of Yamaraja, the Lord of
Death, to seek thee?". . .

But like a mist the child passed from his
embrace, and answered, with a wonder in his
eyes : "*I know thee not!*". . .

Then, kneeling in tears before the boy, the
Brahman cried : " O sweetest son, hast thou indeed forgotten the father who loved thee more
than his own life, — who taught thy infant lips to
utter the holy prayers, — who denied thee no wish
of thy heart, bringing thee up as the son of a
rajah, teaching thee all the wisdom of the Brah-

mans? Hast thou forgotten thy mother, also, who weeps for thee now all alone, seeing that I have journeyed so long to find thee? Nay! look at me with thy eyes! look at me again, that thou mayst know me! Or is it because my grief hath so changed me that I am no longer the same in thy sight?" . . .

But the child ever replied : " I know thee not ! "

Then, casting himself upon the ground, the Brahman wept as one smitten by infinite despair, and so sobbed, until the child, touching him, spoke again : " I know thee not ! Thou art to me a stranger ! I know, indeed, that thou art foolish, — uttering the terms *father* and *mother*, signifying conditions that pass away like the grass of the earth. I perceive, also, that thou art sorrowful, and therefore a victim of delusion ; for sorrow springeth from ignorance and desire, as the fungus from corruption. Here we know not desire, we know not sorrow, neither do we harbor illusion. Thou art no more to me than the wind to the moon, than the flame blown out is to the object once illuminated. Get thee from hence, therefore, as it will profit thee nothing to bring thy sorrow and thy folly into this place.". . .

So the Brahman departed, speechless for grief.

⁎

Only then did he seek the Buddha (the Shahman Gotama,) that he might obtain advice and consolation. And the Buddha, pitying him, laid his hand upon his heart, and gave him rest saying : —

" O Brahman, thou hast only been punished for thy self-delusion and folly.

" Know that the spirit of the dead receiveth a new bodily form after its departure, so that former relationship utterly ceaseth, even as one visiting a tavern by the wayside is no longer a guest, having departed therefrom.

" Much thou art to be pitied for thy weakness and this delusion of thy love, nor canst thou find consolation but in supreme wisdom only.

" Vainly do men concern themselves regarding wife and child ; for the end cometh to all as a roaring torrent, sweeping away whatsoever earthly affection clings to.

" Then neither father nor mother can save ; then neither love nor strength may succor ; parent and kinsman become as blind men set to guard a burning lamp.

" Therefore the truly wise considereth not such things, seeking only to save the world, to enlighten men, to destroy sorrow by destroying desire, to redeem himself.

"Even as the wind driveth away clouds, so should the wise seek to banish thought, to banish worldly consciousness, and thus escape forever the future birth and death, attaining the eightfold Wisdom, — finding at last the eternal peace, the eternal rest.

"Whatsoever is high shall be brought low; wheresoever is agreement will surely come division; where there is birth there shall surely be death also.

"Therefore cast off, O Brahman, all passion, all affection, all regret, as the Vassika plant sheds its withered flowers; therefore flee the ignorant, and seek in solitude the true wisdom, needing no companion, rejoicing as the elephant escaped from the herd. . . ."

And, perceiving the vanity of life, the evanescence of joy, the folly of grief, that Brahman ceased to mourn, and besought permission to follow the footsteps of the Teacher. . . .

THE LOTOS OF FAITH;

Or, " The Furnace of Fire," which is in the JATAKAS *of Buddha. . . . At his birth the waters of the Sea became fresh, and the deeps of the Seven Hells were illuminated. The blind received their sight, that they might behold the bliss of the world ; the deaf their hearing, that they might know the tidings of joy ; by sevenfold lotos-flowers the rocks were riven asunder ; the light of glory immeasurable filled the world systems of ten thousand suns. . . .*

In the years when Brahmadatta reigned over Benares, — the holy city, — the city of apes and peacocks, — the city possessing the seven precious things, and resounding with the ten cries, with the trumpeting of elephants, the neighing of horses, the melody of instruments and voices of singing girls, — then the future Buddha-elect was born as a son in the family of the royal treasurer, after having passed through kotis of births innumerable.

Now the duration of one koti is ten millions of years.

And the Buddha-elect, the Bodisat, was brought up in splendid luxury as a prince of the holy city, and while yet a boy mastered all branches of human knowledge, and becoming a

man succeeded his father as keeper of the treasury.   But even while exercising the duties of
his office, he gave rich gifts to holy men, and
allowed none to excel him in almsgiving.

At that time there also lived a holy Buddha,
who, striving to fulfil each and all of the Ten
Perfections, had passed seven days and seven
nights without eating so much as one grain of
rice.   Arousing himself at last from his holy
trance, he cleansed and robed his person, and
purified himself, and passing through the air by
virtue of his perfection, alighted before the door
of the treasurer's house, with his begging-bowl
in his hand.

Then the Bodisat, beholding the sacred mendicant awaiting in silence, bade a servant fetch to
him the Buddha's bowl, that he might fill it with
such food as those who seek supreme wisdom
may permit themselves to eat.   So the servant
proceeded to fetch the bowl.

But even as he advanced, and before he might
reach out his hand, the ground rocked and heaved
like the sea beneath him ; and the earth opened
itself, and yawned to its entrails, making an abyss
between the holy mendicant and the servant of
the Bodisat.   And the gulf became a hell of seeth-
ing flame, like the hell of Avici, like the heart of

a volcano in which even the crags of granite melt as wax, pass away as clouds. Also a great and fantastic darkness grew before the sun, and blackened all his face.

Wherefore the servant and his fellows fled shrieking, leaving only the Bodisat standing upon one verge of the abyss, and the Buddha, calmly waiting, upon the other. Where the feet of the perfect mendicant stood, the abyss widened not; but it widened swiftly, devouring the ground before the feet of the Bodisat, as though seeking to engulf him. For Mara, Lord of Rakshasas and of evil ones, desiring that the Buddha might die, sought thus to prevent the almsgiving of the Bodisat. And the darkness before the sun was the darkness of Mara's awful face.

And as a muttering of mountain thunder came a voice, saying: "The Buddha shall not live by thine alms-gift; his hour hath come. . . . Mine is the fire between thee and him."

And the Bodisat looked at the Buddha across the abyss of fire; and the Buddha's face changed not, neither did he utter a word to dissuade nor give one sign to encourage.

But the Bodisat cried aloud, even while the abyss, widening, grew vaster to devour him: "Mara, thou shalt not prevail! To thee power

is not given against duty! . . . My lord Buddha,
I come to thee, fearing not; take thou this food
from the hands of thy servant."

And with the dish of rice in his hands, the Bodisat strode into the roaring waste of fire, uttering these jewel-words: *"Better to enter willingly
into hell than neglect a duty or knowingly commit a wrong!"*. . .

Even then the Buddha smiled on the other
verge. And ere the Bodisat could fall, there
suddenly arose from the depths of the pit of
fire a vast and beautiful lotos-flower, like unto
that from whose womb of gold was Brahma born;
and it received the feet of the Bodisat, and bore
him beyond the pit, upcasting over him a spray
of golden dust, like a shower of stars. So he
poured into the Buddha's bowl the holy gift of
alms.

The darkness vanished; the abyss was not;
the Buddha, rising in air, passed over a bridge
of rosy cloud to the mountain regions of Hima-
laya. But the Bodisat, still standing upon the
lotos of gold, long discoursed unto the people
concerning holy things.

RUNES FROM THE KALEWALA.

THE MAGICAL WORDS.

There is in the ancient Finnish tongue a strange book written, called KALEWALA, *a book of runes, treating about the beginning of the world, and about the god-smiths who first wrought the foundations of the sky, and about the witches and the enchanters of the farthest North. Of witches Louhi was among the greatest; and her daughter was wooed by gods and heroes, — even by Wainamoinen the mightiest. . . . So fair was the virgin that her beauty gave light like the moon; so white were her bones that their whiteness glimmered through the transparency of her flesh; so clear was the ivory of her bones that the marrow could be seen within them. . . . And the story of how Wainamoinen built a boat that he might sail to woo the virgin, is thus told in the runes of the* KALEWALA : —

. . . The aged and valiant Wainamoinen resolved to build himself a boat, a swift war-boat. He hewed the trees, he hewed the trunks of the pines and the firs, singing songs the while, chanting the runes that banish evil. And as he sang the smitten trees answered him, the fibres of the

oak and of the fir and of the mountain pine
yielded up their secrets in sounds that to other
men seemed echoes only, but which to Wainamoinen's ears were syllables and words, — words
wrung from the wood by enchantment.

Now only the keel remained to be wrought;
the strong keel of the war-ship had yet to be
fashioned.   And Wainamoinen smote down a
great oak, that he might carve and curve its
body as keels are curved and carven.   But the
dying oak uttered its words of wood, its magical
voice of warning, saying: "Never may I serve
for the keel of thy boat, for the bottom of thy
war-ship.   Lo ! the worms have made their
crooked dwellings within my roots : yesterday
the raven alighted upon my head; bloody was
his back, bloody his crest, and blood lay clotting
upon the blackness of his neck."

Therefore the ancient Wainamoinen left the
oak, and sought among the mountain firs and
the mountain pines for flawless keel-wood ; and
he found wood worthy of his war-boat, and he
wrought the same into shape by the singing of
magical songs.

For the words of enchantment by which shapes
are shaped were known to him ; by magical words
he had wrought the hull, with magical words had

formed the oars; and ribs and keel were by wizard song interlocked together. But to perfect the prow three words must be sung, three warlock words; and those three words Wainamoinen did not know, and his heart was troubled because he did not know them.

There was a shepherd dwelling among the hills, — an ancient shepherd who had beheld ten times a hundred moons; and him Wainamoinen questioned concerning the three magical words.

But the ancient shepherd answered him dreamily: "Surely thou mayst find a hundred words, a thousand syllables of magical song, upon the heads of the swallows, upon the shoulders of the wild geese, upon the necks of the swans!"

Then the aged and valiant Wainamoinen went forth in search of the magical words. He slew the flying swallows by thousands; thousands of white geese he slew; thousands of snowy swans were stricken by his arrows. Yet he found no word written upon their heads, their shoulders, their necks, nor even so much as the beginning of a word. Then he thought unto himself: "Surely I may find a hundred words, a thousand syllables of song, under the tongues of the summer reindeer, within the ruddy mouth of the white squirrel."

And he went his way to seek the magical words. He strewed the vast plains with the bodies of slaughtered reindeer ; he slew the white squirrels by thousands and tens of thousands. But he found no word beneath the tongue of the reindeer, no magical word in the mouth of the white squirrel, not even so much as the beginning of a word.

* *

Yet again Wainamoinen thought to himself, saying : " Surely I may find a hundred magical words, a thousand syllables of song, in the dwelling of the Queen of Death, in the land of Tuonela, in the underground plains of Manala."

And he took his way unto the dwelling-place of Tuonela, to the moonless land of the dead, to the underground plains of Manala. Three days he journeyed thither with steps lighter than air ; three days he journeyed as a shadow walking upon shadow.

And he came at last unto the banks of the sacred river, the sable shore of the black river, over which the spirits of the dead must pass ; and he cried out to the children of Death : " O daughters of Tuoni, bring hither your bark ! O children of Manala, bring hither your bark, that I may cross over the black river ! "

But the daughters of Death, the children of Hell, cried out, saying: " The bark shall be taken over to thee only when thou shalt have told us how thou hast come to Manala, how thou hast reached Tuonela, — the abode of Death, the domain of ghosts."

And Wainamoinen called out to them across the waters, saying: " Surely Tuoni himself hath conducted me hither; surely the Queen of Death hath driven me to Tuonela."

But the daughters of Tuonela waxed wroth; the virgins of Kalma were angry. And they answered: " We know the artifice of men; we perceive the lie within thy mouth. For surely thou livest! no wound hath slain thee; no woe hath consumed thee; no disaster hath destroyed thee; no grave hath been dug for thee. Who, therefore, hath brought thee alive to Manala?"

And Wainamoinen, answering, called out to them across the waters: ' Iron surely hath brought me to the land of death; steel surely hath accompanied me unto Manala."

The daughters of Tuonela waxed wroth; the virgins of Kalma were angry. And they answered: " We know all artifices of men; we perceive the lie within thy mouth. Had iron brought thee to Tuonela, had steel accompanied thee unto Manala, thy garments would drip with blood. . . . Who brought thee to Manala?"

And Wainamoinen called out again to them across the waters: "Fire hath brought me unto Manala; flame hath accompanied me to Tuonela."

The daughters of Tuonela waxed wroth; the virgins of Kalma were angry. And they cried out: "We know all artifices of men; we perceive the lie within thy mouth. Had fire brought thee to Manala, had flame accompanied thee to Tuonela, thy garments would be consumed by the fire, the glow of the flame would be upon thee. Who brought thee to Manala?"

And Wainamoinen yet again called out to them across the black river, saying: "Water hath brought me to Manala; water hath accompanied me to Tuonela."

The daughters of Tuonela waxed wroth; the virgins of Kalma were angry. And they answered, saying: "We know all the artifices of men; we perceive the lie within thy mouth. For there is no dripping of water from thy garments. Cease, therefore, to lie to us; for we know thou livest; we perceive that no wound hath slain thee, no woe consumed thee, no disaster hath crushed thy bones. Who brought thee to Manala? who guided thee to Tuonela?"

Then Wainamoinen called out to them across the river : " Surely I will now utter the truth. I have made me a boat by my art; I have wrought me a war-boat by magical song. With a song I shaped the hull; with a song I formed the keel; with a song I fashioned the oars. Yet three words are wanting to me, — three magical words by which I may perfect the carven prow in its place ; and I have come to Tuonela to find these three words ; I have come to Manala to seek these three words of enchantment. Bring hither your bark, O children of Tuonela! bring hither your boat, O virgins of Kalma! "

So the daughters of Death came over the dark river in their black boat, and they rowed Waina-moinen to the further shore, to the waste of wandering ghosts ; and they gave him to drink of what the dead drink, and to eat of what the dead devour. And Wainamoinen laid him down and slept, being weary with his mighty journey.

He slept and dreamed ; but his garments slept not, — his enchanted garments kept watch for him.

***

Now the daughter of Tuoni, the iron-fingered daughter of Death, seated herself in the darkness upon a great stone in the midst of the waters ;

and with iron fingers wove a net of iron thread, one thousand ells in length.

The sons of Tuoni, the sons of the Queen of Death, also seated themselves in the same darkness upon the same great stone in the midst of the same waters, and with their hookéd fingers, with their iron finger-nails, also wove a net of iron thread, a thousand ells in length.

And they cast their net into the river, across the river, that they might ensnare Wainamoinen, that they might entangle the magician, that they might prevent him from ever leaving the abyss of Manala, ever leaving the domain of Tuonela, so long as the golden moon should circle in heaven, even so long as the silver sun should light the world of men.

But the garments of Wainamoinen kept watch, the enchanted garments of the magician slept not. And Wainamoinen uttered a magical word, and changed himself into a stone; and the stone rolled into the black river.

And the stone became a viper of iron, and passed sinuously through the meshes of the nets, and through the river currents, and into the black reeds upon the black river's further bank.

So Wainamoinen passed from the kingdom of Tuoni, from the children of Death; but he had not found the magical words, nor so much as the part of a word.

* *

Then thought Wainamoinen unto himself: "Surely I may find a hundred words, a thousand syllables of song, in the mouth of the earth-giant, in the entrails of the ancient Kalewa! Long is the way to his resting-place; one must travel awhile over the points of women's needles, and awhile upon the sharp edges of warriors' swords, and yet again awhile upon the sharp steel of the battle-axes of heroes."

And Wainamoinen went to the forge of his brother Ilmarinnen, — Ilmarinnen, the Eternal Smith, who forged the vault of heaven, leaving no mark of the teeth of the pincers, no dent of the blows of the hammer, — Ilmarinnen, who forged for men during the age of darkness a sun of silver and a moon of gold. And he cried out: "O Ilmarinnen, mighty brother, forge me shoes of iron, gloves of iron, a coat of iron! forge me a staff of iron with a pith of steel, that I may wrest the magic words from the stomach of Kalewa, from the dead entrails of the earth-giant."

And Ilmarinnen forged them. Yet he said: "O brother Wainamoinen, the ancient Kalewa is dead; the grave of the earth-giant is deep. Thou mayst obtain no word from him, — not even the beginning of a word."

But Wainamoinen departed; Wainamoinen hastened over the way strewn with the points of needles and the edges of swords and axe-heads of sharpest steel. He ran swiftly over them with shoes of iron; he tore them from his path with gloves of iron, until he reached the resting-place of Kalewa, the vast grave of the earth-giant.

For a thousand moons and more Kalewa had slept beneath the earth. The poplar-tree, the *haapa*, had taken root upon his shoulders; the white birch, the *koivu*, was growing from his temples; the elder tree, the *leppa*, was springing from his cheeks; and his beard had become overgrown with *pahju*-bark, with the bark of the drooping willow. The shadowy fir, the *oravikuusi*, was rooted in his forehead; the mountain-pine, the *havukonka*, was sprouting from his teeth; the dark spruce, the *petaja*, was springing from his feet.

But Wainamoinen tore the haapa from his shoulders, and the koivu from his temples, and the leppa from his cheeks, and the pahju-bark from his beard, and the oravikuusi from his forehead, and the havukonka from his teeth, and the petaja from his feet.

Then into the mouth of the Mountain-breaker, into the mouth of the buried giant, Wainamoinen mightily thrust his staff of smithied iron.

And Kalewa awoke from his slumber of ages, — awoke with groans of pain, — and he closed his jaws upon the staff; but his teeth could not crush the core of steel, could not shatter the staff of iron. And as Kalewa opened wider his mouth to devour the tormentor, lo! Wainamoinen leaped into the yawning throat and descended into the monstrous entrails. And Wainamoinen kindled a flame in the giant's belly, — built him a forge in his entrails.

Then Kalewa, in his great agony, called on that god who leans upon the axis of the world, and upon the blue goddesses of the waters, and upon the deities of the icy wildernesses, and upon the spirits of the forest, and even upon the great Jumala, at whose birth the brazen mountains trembled and lakes were changed into hills. But the gods came not to aid him.

Then Kalewa cursed his tormentor with a thousand magical curses, — with curses of wind and storm and fire, — with curses that change men's faces into stone, — with curses that transport the accursed to the vast deserts of Laponia, where the hoof of the horse is never heard, where the children of the mare can find no pasturage. But the curses harmed not Wainamoinen; the curses only called forth the laughter of scorn from the lips of Wainamoinen.

And Wainamoinen cried out unto Kalewa: "Never shall I depart from hence, O thou mightiest singer of runes, until I have learned from thee the three magical words which I desire, — the three words of enchantment that I have sought throughout the world in vain. Sing to me, O Kalewa, thy songs, thy most wondrous songs, thy marvellous songs of enchantment."

So the giant Kalewa, the possessor of sublimest wisdom, the singer of marvellous runes, opened his mouth and sang his songs for Wainamoinen, — his most wondrous songs, his wizard songs.

Words succeeded to words, verses to verses, wizard runes to wizard runes. Ere Kalewa could sing all that he knew, could utter all that he had learned, the mountains would cease to be, the waters of the rivers would dry up, the great lakes be depopulated of their finny people, the sea have forgotten its power to make waves.

Unceasingly he sang for many days, unceasingly for many sleepless nights; he sang the songs of wizards, the songs of enchantment, the songs that create or destroy.

He sang the songs of wisdom, the runes sung by the gods before the beginning of the world, the verses by whose utterance nothingness became substance and darkness became light.

And as he sang the fair Sun paused in her course to hear him; the golden Moon stopped in her path to listen; the awful billows of the sea stood still; the icy rivers that devour the pines, that swallow up the firs, ceased to rage; the mighty cataracts hung motionless above their abysses; the waves of Juortana lifted high their heads to hear.

And Wainamoinen heard at last the three words, the three magical words, he sought for; and he ceased tormenting Kalewa, and departed from him. So Kalewa sank again into his eternal slumber, and the earth that loved him recovered him, and the forests rewove their network of knotted roots above his place of sleep. . . .

THE FIRST MUSICIAN.

In the ancient runes of the Finns, the runes of the KALEWALA, *is related the creation of the world from the yolk of an egg, and of the heavens from the shell of the egg ; also the origin of Iron and the birth of Steel and the beginning of Music. . . . Now the first musician was no other than Wainamoinen ; and the first kantele, triple-stringed, was made by him from the resonant wood of the fir, and from the bones of a giant pike, as is told in the Twenty-second Rune. Out of the fir-tree was formed the body of the kantele ; out of the teeth of the pike-fish were the screws wrought ; and the strings were made of hairs from the black mane of the steed of Hiisi the magician, — from the shining mane of the stallion of Hiisi, the herder of wolves and bears. . . .*

. . . So the instrument was completed, the kantele was prepared ; and the aged and valiant Wainamoinen bade the old men to play upon it, and to sing the runes of old.

And they sang, but wearily, as winds in mountain wastes ; and their voices trembled frostily, and the instrument rebelled against the touch of their feeble fingers.

Then the ancient and valiant Wainamoinen commanded the young men to sing. But their fingers became cramped upon the strings, and the sounds called forth were sorrowful, and the instrument rebelled against their touch. Joy

answered not unto joy, song responded not unto
song.

Then the ancient and valiant Wainamoinen
sent the kantele to the wizard people who dwelt
in the wastes of ice, to the people of Pohjola, to
the Witch of Pohjola.

And the Witch sang, and the witch-virgins
with her; the wizards also, and the children of
the wizards. But joy answered not unto joy;
song responded not unto song. And the kantele shrieked beneath the touch of their fingers,
shrieked like one who, fearing greatly in the
blackness of the night, feeleth invisible hands
upon him.

Then spake an aged man who had seen more
than two hundred winters, — an ancient man
aroused by the shrieking of the kantele from
his slumber within the recess of the hearth:
"Cease! cease! for the sounds which ye utter
make anguish in my brain, the noises which ye
make do chill the marrow within my bones.
Let the instrument be cast into the waters, or
returned forthwith unto him who wrought it."

Then from the strings of the kantele issued
sweet sounds, and the sounds shaped themselves
into words, and the kantele answered with its
voice, praying: "Cast me not into the deep, but

return me rather unto him who wrought me ; for in the hands of my creator I will give forth sounds of joy, I will utter sounds of harmonious sweetness."

So they took back the kantele unto Waina- moinen, who had wrought it.

* * *

And the ancient and valiant Wainamoinen washed his thumbs ; he purified his fingers ; he seated himself by the sea upon the Stone of Joy, upon the Hillock of Silver, even at the summit of the Hill of Gold ; and he took the instrument within his hands, and lifted up his voice, saying : " Let him that hath never heard the strong joy of runes, the sweet sound of instruments, the sound of music, come hither and hear ! "

And the ancient Wainamoinen began to sing Limpid his voice as the voice of running water, deep and clear, mighty and beautiful.

Lightly his fingers ran over the strings of the kantele ; and the kantele sang in answer, — sang weirdly, sang wondrously, sang throbbingly, like the throats of a thousand birds. And its joy answered unto the joy of the singer ; its song responded unto Wainamoinen's song.

All the living creatures of the forest, all the living creatures of air, drew nigh unto the rune-

singer, gathered themselves about the mighty
chanter, that they might hear the suavity of his
voice, that they might taste the sweetness of his
song.

The gray wolves came from their lurking-places
in the vast marshes; the bears deserted their
dwellings under the roots of the firs, within the
hollows of the giant pines; and they clambered
over the hedges in their way, they broke down
the obstacles before them. And the wolves
mounted upon the heights, the bears upon the
trees, while Wainamoinen called Joy into the
world, while Wainamoinen sang his wondrous
song.

The lord of the forest, also, the old man of
the black beard, — Knippana, king of the joyous
woods; and all the followers of Tapio, god of
wild creatures, came forth to hear, and were visible. Even the wife of the forest king, the goddess of savage beasts, the mistress of Tapiola,
donned her raiment of red, and put on her azure
stockings, and ascended a hollow birch that she
might lend ear to the songs of the god.

All animals of the woods, all birds of the air,
hurried to hear the marvellous art of the musician,
hastened to taste the sweetness of his song.

The eagle descended from the clouds; the fal-

con clave the airs; the white gulls rose from the
far sea-marshes, the swans from the clear deeps
of running water; the swift lark, the quick finch,
the comely linnet, came to perch upon the shoulders of the god.

The Sun, bright virgin of the sky, — the Sun,
rich in her splendors, — and the fair-shining Moon,
had paused in their paths; the first upon the
luminous vault of heaven, the other upon the end
of a long cloud. There were they weaving their
subtle tissues of light, — weaving with shuttle of
gold, carding with carding-comb of silver. Suddenly they heard the unknown voice of song, —
the voice, mighty and sweet, of the rune-singer.
And the shuttle of gold escaped from their hands,
and the carding-comb of silver slipped from their
fingers, and the threads of their tissue were
broken.

All animals living in the waters, all the thou-
sand-finned fishes of the deep, came to hear the
voice of Wainamoinen, came to taste the sweetness of his song.

Swiftly came the salmon and the trout, the
pikes also and the sea-dogs; all the great fishes
and all the little fishes swam toward the shore,
and remained as nigh as they might remain, and
lifted their heads to listen.

And Ahto, monarch of waters, — Ahto, ancient as the ocean, and bearded with water-weeds, — arose upon his great water-lily above the waves.

The fertile wife of the sea-god was combing her hair with a comb of gold, and she heard the voice of the singer. And the comb fell from her hands; trembling of pleasure seized her, torture of desire came upon her to hear, so that she arose from the green abyss and approached the shore. There, leaning with her bosom upon the rock, she listened to the sounds of the kantele, mingling with the voice of Wainamoinen, — so tender the sounds, so sweet the song!

All the heroes wept; the hardest of hearts were softened; there were none of all having never wept before who did not weep then.

The youths wept; the old men wept; the strong men wept; the virgins wept; the little infants wept; even Wainamoinen also felt the source of his own tears rising to overflow.

And soon his tears began to fall, outnumbering the wild berries of the hills, the heads of the swallows, the eggs of the fowls.

They streamed upon his cheeks; and from his cheeks they fell upon his knees, and from his knees they dropped upon his feet, and from his feet they rolled into the dust.

And his tear-drops passed through his six gar-ments of wool, his six girdles of gold, his seven robes of blue, his eight tunics all thickly woven.

And the tears of Wainamoinen flowed as a river, and became a river, and poured themselves to the shores of the sea, and precipitated themselves from the shores into the deeps of the abyss, into the region of black sands.

There did they blossom ; there were they trans-formed into pearls, — pearls destined for the crowns of kings, for the eternal joy of noblest heroes.

.**

And the aged Wainamoinen cried out : " O youths, O daughters of illustrious race ! is there none among ye who will go to gather up my tears from the deeps of the ocean, from the region of black sand ? "

But the youths and the elders answered, say-ing : " There is none among us willing to go to gather up thy tears from the deeps of the ocean, from the region of black sand."

Then a seamew, a seamew with plumage of blue, dipped her beak into the cold waves ; and she gathered the pearls, and she gathered the tears, of Wainamoinen from the deeps of the ocean, from the region of black sand.

THE HEALING OF WAINAMOINEN.

... " She is all fair, the Goddess of Veins, — the Goddess Suonetar, the beneficent Goddess of Veins. Marvellously doth she spin the veins of men with her wondrous spindle, with her distaff of brass, with her spinning-wheel of iron.". ..

LIKE the leaping of the mountain stream, like the rushing of a torrent, the blood issued from the knee of Wainamoinen, wounded by his own axe through the craft of Hiisi the Evil, through the malice of Lempo, the herder of wolves and bears.

The ancient and valiant Wainamoinen had knowledge of all wisdom, all speech that is eternal, all magical words save only the word by which wizard wounds are healed. He invoked the magical art, he uttered the awful imprecation; carefully he read the Original Words, pronounced the runes of science.

But he had forgotten the mightiest words, — the Words of Blood, the charmed words by which the palpitant torrent is checked, by which the gory stream is held back, by which invincible dikes are cast athwart the places broken by iron, athwart the bites made by the blue teeth of steel.

And the blood ceased not to gush bubbling from the wound of the hero, from the knee of Wainamoinen.

***

The aged and valiant Wainamoinen harnessed his steed to his brown sledge ; he mounted upon the seat, smote the swift horse, and cracked his great whip adorned with pearls.

The steed flew over the long course, drawing the brown sledge, devouring distance. Swift as wind was the driving of Wainamoinen, until he neared the dwelling of the sorcerers, the first of the habitations of the wizards. And he halted at the threshold, and cried: " Is there in this habitation any man learned in the knowledge of iron, — any man who can oppose a dike to this river, who can check this torrent of blood?"

A child, a little child, was seated in the middle of the floor; and the child answered, saying: " There is no man here learned in the knowledge of iron, — no man able to assuage with his breath even the bruises of wood, nor to ease the pain of heroes. . . . Go thou to another habitation."

The ancient and valiant Wainamoinen made his great whip, adorned with pearls, whistle upon the flanks of his rapid courser. Swift as lightning his course, until they came to the middle dwelling; and Wainamoinen halted at the threshold, and cried aloud: "Is there in this habitation any man learned in the knowledge of iron, — any man able to oppose a dike to this river, to check this torrent of blood?"

An aged woman was there, lying under her blankets, chattering, babbling, within the furthest end of the recess of the hearth, — an aged woman with three teeth only, — the wisest woman in all that country. And she arose and drew nigh unto the door, and made reply, saying: "There is no man here learned enough to comprehend the misfortune of the hero, to ease his pain, to stop the river of the veins, the rainfall of blood, the torrent of blood out-rolling. Go, seek thou such a man in some other habitation."

The aged and valiant Wainamoinen made his great whip, adorned with pearls, whistle upon the flanks of his swift steed. Lightning-wise he followed the long way leading to the highest habitation. And he descended at the threshold, and leaning against a pillar, cried aloud: "Is there in this habitation any man learned in the knowledge of iron, — any man able to oppose a dike to this river, to check this torrent of blood?"

An aged man dwelt within the great fireplace. His voice roared from the recess of the glowing hollow : " We have checked mightier ones, we have enchained swifter ones, we have overcome greater dangers, we have broken down loftier obstacles, — even by the Three Words of the Creator, by the utterance of the Original Words, the holy words. By them the mouths of rivers, the courses of lakes, the fury of cataracts, have been overcome. We have separated straits from promontories ; we have conjoined isthmuses with isthmuses."

*

The aged Wainamoinen descended from his sledge, and entered beneath the old man's roof. A cup of silver was brought to him, and a cup of gold ; but these could not contain the least part of the blood of Wainamoinen, the blood of the noble god.

The old man roared from the recess of the hearth, — the long-beard cried out : " What manner of man art thou? what hero? Already have seven cups, eight great vessels, been filled with the blood flowing from thy knee ! Ah ! would I could utter other magical words, — even the great Words of Blood ! But, alas ! I have forgotten the origin of Iron."

Then said the aged Wainamoinen : " I know the origin of Iron ; I know the birth of Steel. There were three children whose origin was the same : Water, which is the eldest ; Iron, which is the youngest ; Fire, to which the middle rank belongs. And Fire soon displayed its rage ; flames lifted themselves insolently, and waxed vast with pride. The fields were consumed, the marshes were scorched in that great year of sterility, in that fatal summer which devoured with inextinguishable fire all creatures of nature. Then did Iron seek a refuge, a place wherein to hide.". . .

The old man roared from the recess of the hearth : " Where did Iron hide itself? Where did it find refuge in that great year of barrenness, in that fatal summer which devoured all creatures of nature ? "

The aged Wainamoinen, the valiant Wainamoinen, made answer : " Then Iron hid itself ; Iron found a refuge in the extremity of a long cloud, in the summit of an oak stripped of its branches, in the budding bosom of a young girl. . . . There were three virgins, three affianced maidens, who poured forth upon the ground the milk of their breasts. The milk of the first was black ; the milk of the second, white ; the milk of the third was ruddy. Of the virgin whose milk was black, Flexible Iron was born ; of her whose milk was white, Fragile Iron was born ; of her

11

with the ruddy milk was born Steel. . . . Then
for two years Iron hid itself in the midst of a
vast marsh, upon the summit of a rock where the
white swans laid their eggs, where the wild duck
hatched out her little ones. And the wolf rushed
through the marsh ; and the bear rushed into the
sterile plain ; and they tore up the earth that concealed the Iron. But a god, passing through that
barren place, saw the black sand that the wolf had
torn up, that the bear had trampled beneath his
feet. . . . And that day the Iron was taken out
of the marsh, and purged from the slime of the
earth, and purified by drying from the humidity
of the waters."

The old man roared from the recess of the
hearth : " So that was the origin of Iron ? that
was the birth of Steel ? "

But the valiant Wainamoinen made answer :
" Nay ! not yet has the origin of Iron been
told. For, without devouring Fire, Iron may not
be born ; without Water, it may not be hardened.
Into the workshop of the great smith it was
borne, into the forge of Ilmarinnen ; and the
mighty craftsman, the Eternal Smith, said unto
it : ' If I place thee within my fire, if I put thee
into the flame of my forge-fire, thou wilt become
arrogant, thou wilt wax strong, thou wilt spread

terror about thee, thou wilt slay thy brother,
thou wilt kill the son of thy mother.'. . . Then
the Iron within the forge fires, under the blows
of the hammer, sware this oath : ' I have trees to
rend, hearts of stone to gnaw ; no! never will I
slay my brother, never will I kill the son of my
mother.'. . . Then did Ilmarinnen soften the Iron
within the heart of the furnace, and shape it upon
the anvil. But ere dipping it into the water, he
tested with his tongue, he tasted with his palate,
the creative juices of Steel, the water that gives
hardness unto Iron. And he cried : ' This water
is powerless to create Steel, to harden Iron. O
Mehilainen, bird of Hiisi! O Herlihainen, my
bird-friend ! fly hither upon thine agile wings ;
fly over the marshes, over the lands, over the
straits of the ocean ! bring me honey upon thy
feathers ; bear to me upon thy tongue the honey
of seven meadow-stalks, of six flower-pistils, for
the Steel I am going to make, for the Iron I wish
to harden.'. . . But Herlihainen, the evil bird of
Hiisi the Evil, brought the venom of blood, the
black juices of a worm that his lizard-eyes had
seen, the hidden poison of the toad ; and he gave
these to Ilmarinnen for the Steel which was being
prepared, the Iron that was to be tempered. And
suddenly the Iron quivered with rage ; it growled ;

it moved; its oath was forgotten; like a dog it swallowed its own oath, and it slew its brother, it murdered the son of its mother.   Even now it plunges into flesh, bites the knees of men, rages so that blood flows and flows and overflows in vast torrents."

The old man roared from the recess of the hearth: " Now I know the origin of Iron, the fatal destiny of Steel!"   And to his memory came back the Original Words, the great Words of Blood; and he cursed the Iron with magical curses, and quelled with caressing speech the panic of the fleeing blood.   And the hurt of the Iron ceased, and the red torrent stayed its flowing.

Then the old man took within his fingers the extremities of the veins, and counted them, and uttered the magical prayer: —

" *All fair is she, the Goddess of Veins, — Suonetar, the beneficent Goddess of Veins. Marvellously doth she spin the veins of men with her beautiful spindle, with her distaff of brass, with her spinning-wheel of iron. . . . Come, O Goddess of Veins! come unto me!   I invoke thy succor, I call thy name! . . . Bring hither in thy bosom a roll of ruddy flesh, a blue skein of veins, that the wound may be filled, that the ends of the veins may be tied!*" . . .

And suddenly the hurt of Wainamoinen was healed : the flesh became firmer than before ; the severed veins were retied, the severed muscles rejoined, the broken bones reknit.

*

And many other wonderful things said and done by the old man within the recess of the hearth are told of in the Fourth Rune of the ancient Kalewala.

اللّٰه

STORIES OF MOSLEM LANDS.

BOUTIMAR, THE DOVE.

. . . Beyond the seas which are known roar the waters of the Tenebrous Ocean that is unknown to mortals. There the long breakers chant an eternal hymn, in tones unlike to the voices of other seas. And in that ocean there is an island, and in that island the Fountain of Youth unceasingly bubbles up from the mystic caverns; and it was that fountain which King Alexander the Two-Horned, vainly sought. Only his general, the Prophet Khader, found it, whereby he became immortal. And of other mortals Solomon only beheld the waters of that fountain, according to the Persian legend written in the nine hundredth year of the Hejira, by the goldsmith of language, Hossein ben Ali, also called El Vaëz u'l Kashifi. And it may be found in the ANVARI SOHEILI, which are " The Lights of Canopus." . . .

IN the Name of the Most Merciful God! . . . I have heard this tradition of Solomon, the unparalleled among kings, for whom all Genii, and Peris, and men, and beasts of earth, and birds of air, and creatures of the deep begirt the loins of their souls with the girdle of obedience, and whose power was measurable only by the hoofs of the horse of the Zephyr, " whose morning course is a month's journey, and whose evening course is also equal to a month's journey, upon the swiftest of earthly steeds."

. . . Now, Solomon being once enthroned upon the summit of the mightiest of mountains, which yet bears his name, — the mountain at once overlooking the plains of Iran and the kingdoms of India, — all the creatures of the universe gathered to do him honor. The birds of heaven formed a living canopy above him, and the spirits of air ministered unto him. And, as a mist rising from the earth, a perfumed cloud shaped itself before him; and from out the cloud reached a hand, fairer than moonlight, holding a diamond cup in which a strange water made jewel-glimmerings, while a voice sweeter than music spake to him from out the cloud, saying: " The Creator of all — be His nature forever glorified and His power forever honored! — hath sent me to thee, O Solomon, with this cup containing the waters of youth and of life without end. And He hath desired thee to choose freely whether thou wilt or wilt not drink of this draught from the Fountain of Youth. Therefore consider well, O Solomon! Wilt thou drink hereof, and live divinely immortal through ages everlasting, or wilt thou rather remain within the prison of humanity? . . . I wait."

Then a deep silence brooded above the place; for Solomon dreamed upon these words, while the perfumed cloud stirred not, and the white hand motionlessly offered the jewel-cup. And so dreaming, he said unto his own heart: " Surely the gold of life is good wherewith to purchase many things at the great market of the Resurrection; the plain of life is a rich soil wherein to plant the spice-trees of eternal felicity; and joyless is the black repose of death. . . . Yet must I ask counsel of the Genii, and the Peris, and the wisest of men, and the beasts of earth, and the birds of air, before I may resolve to drink."

Still the moon-white hand offered the scintillating cup, and the perfumed cloud changed not. Then the Genii, and the Peris, and the wisest of men, and the beasts of earth, and the birds of heaven, all speaking with one voice of agreement, prayed him that he should drink, inasmuch as the well-being of the world reposed upon his living wisdom, and the happiness of all creatures was sustained by the circle of his life as a jewel held within the setting of a ring of gold.

So that Solomon indeed put out his hand, and

took the cup from the luminous fingers; and the fingers withdrew again into the odorous cloud. Wondrous were the lights within the water; and there was a glow of rosiness unbroken all about the cup, as of the sempiternal dawn in those islands beyond the Ocean of Shadows, where the sun rises never above the east and there is neither night nor day. But hesitating yet once more before he drank, he questioned again the creatures of the universe, asking: "O ye administering Genii and Peri beings, ye wisest among wise men, ye creatures also of air and of earth, say if there be absent from this assembly even one representative of all over whom I hold dominion!"

And they replied: "Master, only Boutimar is not here, — Boutimar the wild dove, most loving of all living creatures."

Then Solomon sent Hudh-hudh to seek the wild dove, — Hudh-hudh, the bird of gold, created by the witchcraft of Balkis, Queen of Sheba, the sorceress of sorceresses; and the golden bird brought back with him Boutimar, the wild dove, most loving of all living creatures. Then it was that Solomon repeated the words of the song which he had written: "O my dove that dwellest in the clifts of the rock, in the secret hiding-places of the

stairs, let me see thy face, let me hear thy voice!
... Is it meet that thy lord, Solomon, shall drink
of the waters of youth and know the bliss of
earthly immortality?"

Then the wild dove, speaking in the tongue of
birds known to Solomon only among mortals,
asked the prophet-king, saying: "How shall a
creature of air answer the source of wisdom? how
may so feeble a mind advise thy supernal intelligence? Yet, if I must counsel, let me ask thee,
O Solomon, whether the Water of Life brought
hither by this perfumed spirit be for thee alone, or
for all with whom thy heart might incline thee to
share it?"

But Solomon answered: "It hath been sent to
only me, nor is there enough within the cup for
any other."

"O prophet of God!" answered Boutimar, in
the tongue of birds, "how couldst thou desire to
be living alone, when each of thy friends and of
thy counsellors and of thy children and of thy
servants and of all who loved thee were counted
with the dead? For all of these must surely
drink the bitter waters of death, though thou
shouldst drink the Water of Life. Wherefore
desire everlasting youth, when the face of the
world itself shall be wrinkled with age, and the

eyes of the stars shall be closed by the black fingers of Azrael? When the love thou hast sung
of shall have passed away like a smoke of frank-
incense, when the dust of the heart that beat
against thine own shall have long been scattered
by the four winds of heaven, when the eyes that
looked for thy coming shall have become a memory, when the voices grateful to thine ear shall
have been eternally stilled, when thy life shall be
one oasis in a universal waste of death, and thine
eternal existence but a recognition of eternal ab-
sence, — wilt thou indeed care to live, though the
wild dove perish when its mate cometh not?"

And Solomon, without reply, silently put out
his arm and gave back the cup, so that the white
hand came forth and took it, and withdrew into
the odorous cloud, and the cloud dissolved and
passed away forever. But upon the prophet-
king's rich beard, besprinkled with powder of
gold, there appeared another glitter as of clear
dew, — the diamond dew of the heart, which is
tears.

THE SON OF A ROBBER.

. . . A bud from the Rose-garden of the Gulistan, planted in the six hundred and fifty-sixth year of the Hejira by the Magician of Speech, the Sheikh Moslih-Eddin Sadi of Shiraz, and arranged after eight divisions corresponding with the Eight Gates of Paradise. . . . In the reign of the King of Kings, Abou-Bequer ben Sad, the Most Magnificent, Viceregent of Solomon, Shadow of the Most High God upon Earth. . . . In the Name of God the Most Merciful.

. . . IN those days there were robbers who dwelt in the mountain regions of the land, having fortresses above the eagle's nests, so that no army might successfully assail them. Their name weighed as a terror upon the land, and they closed up the ways of the caravans, and wasted the valleys, and overcame even the king's troops by their strength and their fierceness, — all being mountain-born and worshippers of devouring fire. So the governors of the mountain provinces held council together, and devised cunning plans by which to allure the robbers from their inaccessible mountain dwelling, so as to destroy them utterly.

Therefore it came to pass that while the robbers were pursuing after a caravan, the bravest troops of the king concealed themselves in the defiles of the mountain, and there in silence awaited the return of the band with many rich spoils and captives of price for ransom. And when the robbers returned at night, hard pressed by that greatest enemy of the wary, whose name is Sleep, the Persian soldiers set upon them, and smote them, and bound their arms behind their backs, and drave them as a herd of wild sheep into the city. So they were brought into the presence of the king.

And the king commended the wisdom of the governors of the provinces, saying: "Had ye not thus prevailed against them by craft, the strength of the robbers might have waxed with each day of immunity, until it would have been beyond our power to destroy them. The spring may be closed at its mouth with a small covering; but when it shall have been swollen to a river by long flowing, a man may not cross its current even upon the back of an elephant. . . . Let each and all of these prisoners be forthwith put to death as robbers are put to death under our law."

But among these robbers there was a youth slender and shapely as a young palm; and the fruit of his adolescence was yet unripe, the verdure of the rose-garden of his cheeks had scarcely begun to bud. And by reason of the beauty of the boy, a kindly vizier bowed his white beard before the steps of the throne, and kissed the footstool of the king, and prayed him with words of intercession : " Hear the prayer of a slave, O Master of the World, Axis of the Circle of Time, Shadow upon Earth of the Most High God ! . . . This child hath never eaten of the fruit of life, never hath he enjoyed the loveliness of the flower of youth. . . . O Master of Kings, thy slave hopes that in thy universal generosity and boundless bounty, thou wilt impose upon thy slave a fresh obligation of gratitude, by sparing the life of this child.". . .

Kindly was the king's heart, but his mind was keen also and clear as edge of diamond ; and he knitted his brows because the discourse seemed to him unwise, and therefore pleased him not: " O vizier, dost thou not know that the influence of the good can make no impression upon the hearts of those whose origin is evil? Hast thou not heard it said that the willow giveth no fruit, however fertilizing the rain of heaven? Shall we extinguish a fire, and leave charcoal embers alight? shall we destroy only the adult viper, and spare her young? It is better that

12

these people be utterly destroyed, root and branch, race and name.". . .

But the aged vizier, bowing respectfully, again prayed the king, justly commending the wisdom of his words, but seeking exceptions and parables from the sayings of the wise and the traditions of the prophets: "The words of the Successor of Solomon are wisdom supreme to thy slave; and were this boy indeed raised up by the wicked, he would surely become as they. Yet thy slave believes that were he educated only by the best of men, he might become most virtuous. Nor would thy slave spare aught requisite to adorn the boy's heart and to make blossom the garden of his mind. . . . The prophetical tradition saith: *There is no child born of woman that is not naturally born into Islam, though his father and mother might afterward make him a Jew, a Christian, or a Gheber.* . . . And even the dog Kitmir, that followed and guarded the Seven Holy Sleepers of Mecca, was able to enter Paradise by seizing with his teeth the hem of their blessed robes.". . .

Then many other ministers and rulers of provinces, unwisely bewitched by the beauty of the boy, united themselves with the vizier in potent intercession. The king's face moved not, and

the shadow remained upon it; but he answered:
"I pardon the boy by reason of the weakness
of your hearts, yet I perceive no advantage
therein. O vizier, bear in mind that the beneficent rains of heaven give radiance to the splendors of the tulip and strength to the venom of
serpent-plants. Remember well that the vilest
enemy may not be despised, and that the stream
now too shallow for the fish may so swell as to
carry away the camel with his burthen.". . .

But the vizier, weeping with joy, took the boy
home, and clothed him and fed him, and brought
him up as his own sons and as the sons of princes.
Masters he procured for him, to make him learned
in the knowledge of tongues and of graces and
of military accomplishments,— in the arts of arch-
ery and sword-play and horsemanship, in singing
and in the musical measurement of speech, in
courtesy and truth, above all things, and those
high qualities desirable in the service of the King
of Kings upon earth. So strong and beautiful
he grew up that the gaze of all eyes followed
whithersoever he moved, even as the waves all
turn their heads to look upon the moon; and
all, save only the king, smiled upon him. But
the king only frowned when he stood before
him, and paid no heed to the compliments ut-

tered concerning the young man. One day, the vizier, in the pride of his happiness, said to the king: "Behold! by the work of thy slave, the boy hath been reclaimed from the ways of his fathers; the fountain of his mind hath been opened by wise teachers, and the garden of his heart blossoms with the flowers of virtuous desire."

But the king only laughed in his beard, and said: "O vizier, the young of the wolf will always be a wolf, even though he be brought up with the children of a man."

***

. . . And when the time of two winters had dimmed the recollection of the king's words, it came to pass at last that the young man, riding out alone, met with a band of mountain robbers, and felt his heart moved toward them. They, also, knowing his race by the largeness and fierceness of his eyes, and the eagle-curve of his nostrils, and the signs of the wild blood that made lightnings in his veins, were attracted to him, and spake to him in the mountain-tongue of his fathers. And all the fierceness of his fathers returned upon him, with longings for the wind-voices of the peaks, and the madness of leaping water, and the sleeping-places above the clouds where the eagles hatched their young, and the secrets of the un-known caverns, and the altar of flickering fire. . . . So that he made compact with them ; and, treach-erously returning, slew the aged vizier together with his sons, and robbed the palace, and fled to the mountains, where he took refuge in his father's ancient fortress, and became a leader of outlaws. And they told the tale to the king.

Then the king, wondering not at all, laughed bitterly and said : "O ye wise fools ! how can a good sword be wrought from bad iron? how may education change the hearts of the wicked? Doth not the same rain which nourisheth the rose also nourish the worthless shrubs that grow in salty marshes? How shall a salty waste produce nard? Verily, to do good unto the evil is not less blame-worthy than to do evil unto the good."

A LEGEND OF LOVE.

Djemil the AZRA *said: " While I live, my heart will love thee; and when I shall be no more, still will my Shadow follow thy Shadow athwart the tombs.".* . .

THOU hast perchance beheld it, — the strong white city climbing by terraces far up the moun-

tain-side, with palms swaying in the blue above
its citadel towers, and the lake-waters damas-
cened by winds, reflecting, all-quiveringly, its
Arabian gates and the golden words of the
Prophet shining upon entablatures, and the
mosque-domes rounded like eggs of the Rok,
and the minarets from which the voice of the
muezzin comes to the faithful with dying red-
ness of sunset: "O ye who are about to sleep,
commend your souls to Him who never
sleeps!"

. . . Therein also dwelt many Christians,—may
their bones be ground and the names of them forever blotted out! Yea; all save one, whose name
I have indeed forgotten. (But our master the
Prophet hath written the name; and it hath not
been forgotten by Him who never forgets, —
though it be the name of a woman!) Now, hard
by the walls of the city there is a place of sepul-
chre for good Moslems, in which thou mayst see
two graves, the foot of one being set against
the foot of the other; and upon one of these
is a monument bearing a turban, while the form
of the tumulary stone upon the other hath only
flowers in relief, and some letters of an obliterated
name, wherefore thou mightst know it to be
the grave of a woman. And there are cypress-

trees more ancient than Islam, making darkness
like a summer's night about the place.

***

. . . Slender she was as the tulip upon its stalk,
and in walking her feet seemed kisses pressed
upon the ground. But hadst thou beheld her
face unveiled, and the whiteness of her teeth between her brown lips when she smiled! . . . He
was likewise in the summer of his youth; and
his love was like the love of the Beni-Azra told of
by Sahid Ben-Agba. But she being a Christian
maiden and he being a good Mussulman, they could
not converse together save by stealth; nor could
either dare to let the matter become known unto
the parents of the other. For he could not indeed
make himself one of the infidel — whose posterity
may God blot out! — neither could she, through
fear of her people, avow the faith of the Prophet!
. . . Only through the lattice of her window could
she betimes converse with him; and with the love
of each other it came to pass that both fell grievously ill. As to the youth, indeed, his sickness
so wrought upon him that his reason departed,
and he long remained as one mad. Then at
last, recovering, he departed to another place,
even to the city of Damascus, — not that he
might so forget what he could not wish to

forget, but that his strength might return to him.

**

Now the parents of the maiden were rich, while the youth was poor. And when the lovers had contrived to send letters one unto the other, she sent to him a hundred dinars, begging him, as he loved her, that he should seek out an artist in that city, and have a likeness of himself painted for her that she might kiss it. "But knowest thou not, beloved," he wrote, "that it is contrary unto our creed; and in the Last Day what wilt thou say unto God when He shall demand of thee to give life unto the image thou hast had wrought?" But she replied: "In the Last Day, O my beloved, I shall answer, Thou knowest, O Most Holy, that Thy creature may not create; yet if it be Thy will to animate this image, I will forever bless Thy name, though Thou condemn me for having loved more than mine own soul the fairest of living images Thou hast made.". . .

**

But it came to pass in time that, returning, he fell sick again in the city which I speak of; and lying down to die, he whispered into the ear of his friend: "Never again in this world shall I behold her whom my soul loveth; and

I much fear, if I die a Mussulman, lest I should not meet her in the other. Therefore I desire to abjure my faith, and to become a Christian." And so he died. But we buried him among the faithful, forasmuch as his mind must have been much disturbed when he uttered those words.

And the friend of the youth hastened with all speed to the place where the young girl dwelt, she being also at the point of death, so grievous was the pain of her heart. Then said she to him: " Never again in this world shall I behold him that my soul loveth; and I much fear if I die a Christian, lest I should not meet him in the other. Therefore I give testimony that there is no other God but God, and that Mahomet is the prophet of God!"

Then the friend whispered unto her what had happened, to her great astonishment. But she only answered: "*Bear me to where he rests; and bury me with my feet toward his feet, that I may rise face to face with him at the Day of Judgment!*"

THE KING'S JUSTICE.

. . . Praise to the Creator of all, the secret of whose existence is unknown; who hath marked all His creatures with an imprint, though there be no visible imprint of Himself; who is the Soul of the soul; who is hidden in that which is hidden! . . . Though the firmament open its myriad million eyes in the darkness, it may not behold Him. Yet does the Sun nightly bow his face of flame below the west, in worship; monthly the Moon faints away in astonishment at His greatness. . . . Eternally the Ocean lifts its thousand waves to proclaim His glory; Fire seeks to rise to Him; Winds whisper of His mystery. . . . And in the balance of His justice even a sigh hath weight. . . .

In the first recital of the First Book of the Gulistan, treating of the Conduct of Kings, it is said that a Persian monarch condemned with his own lips a prisoner of war, and commanded that he be put to death.

And the prisoner, being still in the force of youth and the fulness of strength, thought within his heart of all the days he might otherwise have lived, of all the beauty he might have caressed, of all the happiness he might have known, of all the hopes unbudded that might have ripened into blossom for him. Thus regretting, and seeing before him only the blind and moonless night of death, and considering that the fair sun would never rise for him again, he cursed the king in the language of malediction of his own country, loudly and with mad passion. For it is a proverb: "Whosoever washeth his hands of life, truly saith all that is within his heart."

Now the king, hearing the vehemence of the man, but nowise understanding the barbaric tongue which he spoke, questioned his first vizier, asking, "What saith the dog?"

But the vizier, being a kindly-hearted man, answered thus: "O Master, he repeateth the words of the Holy Book, the words of the Prophet of God concerning those who repress their anger and pardon injury, the beloved of Allah."

And the king, hearing and believing these words, felt his heart moved within him; the fire of his anger died out, and the spirit of pity entered into him, so that he revoked his own command and forgave the man, and ordered that he should be set free.

But there was another vizier also with the king, a malevolent and cunning-eyed man, knowing all languages, and ever seeking to obtain elevation by provoking the misfortune of others. This vizier, assuming therefore an austere face like to that of a praying dervish, loudly exclaimed: "Ill doth it become trusted ministers of a king, men

of honorable place, such as we are, to utter in the
presence of our master even so much as one syl-
lable of untruth.   Know, therefore, O Master,
that the first vizier hath untruthfully interpreted
the prisoner's words ; for that wretch uttered no
single pious word, but evil and blasphemous language concerning thee, cursing his king in the
impotency of his rage."

But the king's brows darkened when he heard
the words ; and turning terrible eyes upon the
second vizier, he said unto him : " More pleasant
to my ears was the lie uttered by my first vizier,
than the truth spoken by thy lips ; for he indeed
uttered a lie with a good and merciful purpose,
whereas thou didst speak the truth for a wicked
and malignant purpose.   Better the lie told for
righteous ends than the truth which provoketh
evil !   Neither shall my pardon be revoked ; but
as for thee, let me see thy face no more ! "

ש"ס

TRADITIONS RETOLD FROM THE TALMUD.

A LEGEND OF RABBA.

Which is in the Gemara of the Berachoth of Babylon. . . . Concerning the interpretation of dreams, it hath been said by Rabbi Benaa: " There were in Jerusalem twenty-four interpreters of dreams; and I, having dreamed a dream, did ask the explanation thereof from each of the twenty-four; and, notwithstanding that each gave me a different interpretation, the words of all were fulfilled, even in conformity with the saying: ' All dreams are accomplished according to the interpretation thereof.' ". . . We are Thine, O King of all; Thine also are our dreams. . . .

MIGHTY was the knowledge of the great Rabba, to whom the mysteries of the Book Yetzirah were known in such wise, that, being desirous once to try his brother, Rabbi Zira, he did create out of dust a living man, and sent the man to Zira with a message in writing. But inasmuch as the man had not been born of woman, nor had had breathed into him God's holy spirit of life, he could not speak. Therefore, when Rabbi Zira had spoken to him and observed that he did not reply, the Rabbi whispered into his ear: " Thou wert begotten by witchcraft; return to thy form of dust!" And the man crumbled before his sight into shapelessness; and the wind bore the shapelessness away, as smoke is dissipated by a breath of storm. But Rabbi Zira marvelled greatly at the power of the great Rabba.

Not so wise, nevertheless, was Rabba as was Bar-Hedia in the interpretation of dreams; and Bar-Hedia was consulted by the multitudes in those parts. But he interpreted unto them good or evil only as they paid him or did not pay him. According to many Rabbonim, to dream of a well signifieth peace; to dream of a camel, the pardon of iniquities; to dream of goats, a year of fertility; to dream of any living creature, save only the monkey and the elephant, is good; and these also are good if they appear harnessed or bound. But Bar-Hedia interpreted such good omens in the contrary way, unless well paid by the dreamer; and it was thought passing strange that the evils which he predicted never failed of accomplishment.

***

Now one day the Rabbonim Abayi and Rabba went to consult Bar-Hedia the interpreter, seeing that they had both dreamed the same dream. Abayi paid him one *zouz*, but Rabba paid him nothing.

And they asked Bar-Hedia, both together saying: "Interpret unto us this dream which we have dreamed. Sleeping, it seemed to us that we beheld a scroll unrolled under a great light, and we did both read therein these words, which are in the fifth book of Moses: "*Thine ox shall be slain before thine eyes, and thou shalt not eat thereof. . . . Thy sons and thy daughters shall be given unto another people. . . . Thou shalt carry much seed out into the field, and shalt gather but little in.*" . . .

Then Bar-Hedia, the interpreter, said to Abayi who had paid him one zouz: "For thee this dream bodeth good. The verse concerning the ox signifies thou wilt prosper so wondrously that for very joy thou shalt be unable to eat. Thy sons and daughters shall be married in other lands, so that thou wilt be separated from them without grief, knowing them to be virtuous and content.

"But for thee, Rabba, who didst pay me nothing, this dream portendeth evil. Thou shalt be afflicted in such wise that for grief thou canst not eat; thy daughters and sons shall be led into captivity. Abayi shall *carry out much seed into the field;* but the second part of the verse, *Thou shalt gather but little,* refers to thee."

Then they asked him again, saying: "But in our dream we also read these verses, thus disposed: *Thou shalt have olive trees, and thou shalt not anoint thyself with oil. . . . All the people of the earth shall see that thou art called by the name of the Lord, and they shall be afraid of thee.*"

Then said Bar-Hedia: "For thee, Rabbi Abayi, the words signify that thou shalt be prosperous and much honored; but for thee, Rabba, who didst pay me nothing, they portend evil only. Thou shalt have no profit in thy labor; thou shalt be falsely accused, and by reason of the accusation, avoided as one guilty of crime."

Still Rabba, speaking now for himself alone, continued: "But I dreamed also that I beheld the exterior door of my dwelling fall down, and that my teeth fell out of my mouth. And I dreamed that I saw two doves fly away, and two radishes growing at my feet."

Again Bar-Hedia answered, saying: "For thee, Rabba, who didst pay me nothing, these things signify evil. The falling of thine outer door augurs the death of thy wife; the loss of thy teeth

signifies that thy sons and daughters shall likewise die in their youth. The flight of the doves
means that thou shalt be divorced from two other
wives, and the two radishes of thy dream fore-
tell that thou wilt receive two blows which thou
mayest not return."

And all things thus foretold by Bar-Hedia came
to pass. So that Rabba's wife died, and that he
was arrested upon suspicion of having robbed the
treasury of the king, and that the people shunned
him as one guilty. Also while seeking to separate two men fighting, who were blind, they struck
him twice unknowingly, so that he could not re-
sent it. And misfortunes came to Rabba even as
to Job; yet he could resign himself to all save
only the death of his young wife, the daughter of
Rabbi Hisda.

*_**

At last Rabba paid a great sum to Bar-Hedia,
and told him of divers awful dreams which he had
had. This time Bar-Hedia predicted happiness
for him, and riches, and honors, all of which came
to pass according to the words of the interpreter,
whereat Rabba marvelled exceedingly.

Now it happened while Rabba and Bar-Hedia
were voyaging one day together, that Bar-Hedia
let fall his magical book, by whose aid he uttered

all his interpretations of dreams; and Rabba, hastily picking it up, perceived these words in the beginning: *All dreams shall be fulfilled according to the interpretation of the interpreter.* So that Rabba, discovering the wicked witchcraft of the man, cursed him, saying: "*Raca!* for all else could I forgive thee, save for the death of my beloved wife, the daughter of Rabbi Hisda! O thou impious magician! take thou my malediction!" . . .

Thereupon Bar-Hedia, terrified, went into voluntary exile among the Romans, vainly hoping thus to expiate his sin, and flee from the consuming power of Rabba's malediction.

*⁎⁎

Thus coming to Rome, he interpreted dreams daily before the gate of the king's treasury; and he did much evil, as he was wont to do before. One day the king's treasurer came to him, saying: " I dreamed a dream in which it seemed to me that a needle had entered my finger. Interpret me this dream."

But Bar-Hedia said only, " Give me a zouz!" And because he would not give it, Bar-Hedia told him nothing.

And another day the treasurer came, saying: " I dreamed a dream in which it seemed that

worms devoured two of my fingers. Interpret
me this dream."

But Bar-Hedia said only, "Give me a zouz!"
And because he would not give it, Bar-Hedia told
him nothing.

Yet the third time the treasurer came, saying:
"I dreamed a dream in which it seemed to me that
worms devoured my whole right hand. Interpret
me this dream."

Then Bar-Hedia mocked him, saying: "Go,
look thou at the king's stores of silk intrusted to
thy keeping; for worms have by this time destroyed them utterly.". . . And it was even as
Bar-Hedia said.

Thereupon the king waxed wroth, and ordered
the decapitation of the treasurer. But he, pro-
testing, said: "Wherefore slay only me, since
the Jew that was first aware of the presence of
the worms, said nothing concerning it?"

So they brought in Bar-Hedia, and questioned
him. But he mocked the treasurer, and said:
"It was because thou wast too avaricious to
pay me one zouz that the king's silk hath been
destroyed."

Whereupon the Romans, being filled with fury,
bent down the tops of two young cedar trees,
one toward the other, and fastened them so

with a rope. And they bound Bar-Hedia's right
leg to one tree-top, and his left leg to the other;
and thereafter severed the rope suddenly with a
sword. And the two cedars, as suddenly leaping
back to their natural positions, tore asunder the
body of Bar-Hedia into equal parts, so that his
entrails were spilled out, and even his skull,
splitting into halves, emptied of its brain.

For the malediction of the great Rabba was
upon him.

———◆———

THE MOCKERS.

*. . . A tradition of Rabbi Simon ben Yochai, which is preserved
within the Treatise Sheviith of the* TALMUD YERUSHALMI. *. . . .
Is it not said in the Sanhedrin that there are four classes who do
not enter into the presence of the Holy One ? — blessed be He ! —
and among these four are scorners reckoned. . . .*

CONCERNING Rabbi Simon ben Yochai many
marvellous things are narrated, both in that Talmud which is of Babylon and in that which is of
Jerusalem. And of these things none are more
wonderful than the tradition regarding the fashion
after which he was wont to rebuke the impudence
of mockers.

It was this same Rabbi Simon ben Yochai, who

was persecuted by the Romans, because he had made little of their mighty works, saying that they had constructed roads only to move their wicked armies more rapidly, that they had builded bridges only to collect tolls, that they had erected aqueducts and baths for their own pleasure only, and had established markets for no other end than the sustenance of iniquity. For these words Rabb Simon was condemned to die; wherefore he, together with his holy son, fled away, and they hid themselves in a cave. Therein they dwelt for twelve long years, so that their garments would have crumbled into dust had they not laid them aside saving only at the time of prayer; and they buried themselves up to their necks in the sand during their hours of slumber and of meditation. But within the cave the Lord created for them a heavenly carob-tree, which daily bore fruit for their nourishment; and the Holy One — blessed be He! — also created unending summer within the cave, lest they should be afflicted by cold. So they remained until the Prophet Elijah descended from heaven to tell them that the Emperor of the Romans had died the death of the idolatrous, and that there remained for them no peril in the world. But during those many years of meditation, the holiness of the Rabbi and of

his son had become as the holiness of those who
stand with faces wing-veiled about the throne of
God ; and the world had become unfitted for their
sojourn.   Coming forth from the cave, therefore,
a fierce anger filled them at the sight of men
ploughing and reaping in the fields ; and they
cried out against them, saying : " Lo ! these people think only of the things of earth, and neglect
the things of eternity."

Then were the lands and the people toiling
thereupon utterly consumed by the fire of their
eyes, even as Sodom and Gomorrah were blasted
from the face of the earth.   But the Bath-Kol —
the Voice of the Holy One — rebuked them from
heaven, saying : " What ! have ye come forth only
to destroy this world which I have made?   Get
ye back within the cavern ! "   And they returned
into the cave for another twelve months, — making in all thirteen years of sojourn therein, — until
the Bath-Kol spake again, and uttered their pardon, and bade them return into the world.   All
of which is written in the Treatise Shabbath of
Seder Moed of the Talmud Babli.

*

Now in the Talmud Yerushalmi we are told
that after Rabbi Simon ben Yochai had departed
from the cave, he resolved to purify all the land

of Tiberias. For while within the cave, his body had become sore smitten with ulcers, and the waters of Tiberias had healed them. Even as he had found purification in Tiberias, so also, he declared, should Tiberias find in him purification. And these things he said within the hearing of mockers, who feared his eyes, yet who among themselves laughed him to scorn.

But Rabbi Simon sat down before the city of Tiberias, and he took lupines, and cut up the lupines into atoms, and uttered over them words whereof no living man save himself knew the interpretation. (For the meaning of such words is seldom known by men, seeing that but few are known even by the Angels and the Demons.) Having done these things, the Rabbi arose and walked over the land, scattering the lupines about him as a sower scatters seed. And wherever the lupines fell, the bones of the dead arose from below and came to the surface of the ground, so that the people could take them away and bury them in a proper place. Thus was the ground purified, not only of the bones of the idolaters and the giants who erst dwelt in the place of promise, but likewise of the bones of all animals and living beings which had there died since the coming of Israel.

Now there was a certain wicked doubter, a Samaritan, who, desiring to bring confusion to Rabbi Simon ben Yochai, secretly buried an unclean corpse in a place already purified. And the Samaritan came cunningly to Rabbi Simon, saying: "Methought thou didst purify such a spot in my field; yet is there an unclean body there, — the body of a man. Surely thy wisdom hath failed thee, or mayhap thy magic hath some defect in it? Come thou with me!" So he took with him Rabbi Simon, and dug up the ground, and showed to him the unclean corpse, and laughed in his beard.

But Rabbi Simon, knowing by divine inspiration what had been done, fixed his eyes upon the wicked face of the man, and said: "Verily, such a one as thou deserveth not to dwell among the living, but rather to exchange places with the dead!" And no sooner had the words been uttered than the body of the dead man arose, and his flesh became pure, and the life returned to his eyes and his heart; while the wicked Samaritan became a filthy corpse, so that the worms came from his nostrils and his ears.

Yet, as he went upon his way, Rabbi Simon passed an inhabited tower without the city; and a voice from the upper chamber of the tower

mocked him, crying aloud: " Hither cometh that
Bar-Yochai, who thinketh himself able to purify
Tiberias ! "   Now the mocker was himself a most
learned man.

" I swear unto thee," answered Rabbi Simon, —
" I swear unto thee that Tiberias shall be made
pure in spite of such as thou, and their mock-
ings."

And even as the holy Rabbi spoke, the mocker
who stood within the chamber of the tower utterly
crumbled into a heap of bones; and from the
bones a writhing smoke ascended, — the smoke
of the wrath of the Lord, as it is written: " *The
anger of the Lord shall smoke !* ". . .

————•————

ESTHER'S CHOICE.

*A story of Rabbi Simon ben Yochai, which is related in the
holy Midrash Shir-Hasirim of the holy Midrashim. . . . Hear,
O Israel, the Lord our God is ONE ! . . . .*

In those days there lived in Sidon, the mighty
city, a certain holy Israelite possessing much
wealth, and having the esteem of all who knew
him, even among the Gentiles. In all Sidon there
was no man who had so beautiful a wife; for the

comeliness of her seemed like that of Sarah, whose loveliness illumined all the land of Egypt.

Yet for this rich one there was no happiness: the cry of the nursling had never been heard in his home, the sound of a child's voice had never made sunshine within his heart. And he heard voices of reproach betimes, saying: " Do not the Rabbis teach that if a man have lived ten years with his wife and have no issue, then he should divorce her, giving her the marriage portion pre-scribed by law; for he may not have been found worthy to have his race perpetuated by her?" . . . But there were others who spake reproach of the wife, believing that her beauty had made her proud, and that her reproach was but the punish-ment of vainglory.

And at last, one morning, Rabbi Simon ben Yochai was aware of two visitors within the ante-chamber of his dwelling, the richest merchant of Sidon and his wife, greeting the holy man with *Salem aleikoum!* The Rabbi looked not upon the woman's face, for to gaze even upon the heel of a woman is forbidden to holy men; yet he felt the sweetness of her presence pervading all the house like the incense of the flowers woven by the hands of the Angel of Prayer. And the Rabbi knew that she was weeping.

Then the husband arose and spake : " Lo ! it is now more than a time of ten years since I was wedded to Esther, I being then twenty years of age, and desirous to obey the teaching that he who remaineth unmarried after twenty transgresseth daily against God. Esther, thou knowest, O Rabbi, was the sweetest maiden in Sidon ; and to me she hath ever been a most loving and sweet wife, so that I could find no fault with her ; neither is there any guile in her heart.

" I have since then become a rich Israelite ; the men of Tyre know me, and the merchants of Carthage swear by my name. I have many ships, bearing me ivory and gold of Ophir and jewels of great worth from the East ; I have vases of onyx and cups of emeralds curiously wrought, and chariots and horses, — even so that no prince hath more than I. And this I owe to the blessing of the Holy One, — blessed be He ! — and to Esther, my wife, also, who is a wise and valiant woman, and cunning in advising.

" Yet, O Rabbi, gladly would I have given all my riches that I might obtain one son ! that I might be known as a father in Israel. The Holy One — blessed be He ! — hath not vouchsafed me this thing ; so that I have thought me found unworthy to have children by so fair and good a woman.

I pray thee, therefore, that thou wilt give legal
enactment to a bill of separation; for I have resolved to give Esther a bill of divorcement, and a
goodly marriage portion also, that the reproach
may so depart from us in the sight of Israel."

***

And Rabbi Simon ben Yochai stroked. thought-
fully the dim silver of his beard. A silence as
of the Shechinah fell upon the three. Faintly,
from afar, came floating to their ears the sea-
like murmuring of Sidon's commerce. . . . Then
spake the Rabbi; and Esther, looking at him,
thought that his eyes smiled, although this holy
man was never seen to smile with his lips. Yet
it may be that his eyes smiled, seeing into their
hearts: " My son, it would be a scandal in Israel
to do as thou dost purpose, hastily and without
becoming announcement; for men might imagine
that Esther had not been a good wife, or thou a
too exacting husband! It is not lawful to give
cause for scorn. Therefore go to thy home, make
ready a goodly feast, and invite thither all thy
friends and the friends of thy wife, and those
who were present at thy wedding, and speak to
them as a good man to good men, and let them
understand wherefore thou dost this thing, and
that in Esther there is no fault. Then return

to me on the morrow, and I will grant thee the
bill."

* * *

So a great feast was given, and many guests
came ; among them, all who had attended the wedding of Esther, save, indeed, such as Azrael had
led away by the hand. There was much good
wine ; the meats smoked upon platters of gold,
and cups of onyx were placed at the elbow of each
guest. And the husband spake lovingly to his
wife in the presence of all, saying : " Esther, we
have lived together lovingly many years ; and if
we must now separate, thou knowest it is not because I do not love thee, but only because it hath
not pleased the Most Holy to bless us with children. And in token that I love thee and wish
thee all good, know that I desire thee to take
away from my house whatever thou desirest,
whether it be gold or jewels beyond price."

* * *

So the wine went round, and the night passed
in mirth and song, until the heads of the guests
grew strangely heavy, and there came a buzzing
in their ears as of innumerable bees, and their
beards ceased to wag with laughter, and a deep
sleep fell upon them.

Then Esther summoned her handmaids, and

said to them : "Behold my husband sleeps heavily! I go to the house of my father; bear him thither also as he sleepeth."

⁂

And awaking in the morning the husband found himself in a strange chamber and in a strange house. But the sweetness of a woman's presence, and the ivory fingers that caressed his beard, and the softness of the knees that pillowed his head, and the glory of the dark eyes that looked into his own awakening, — these were not strange; for he knew that his head was resting in the lap of Esther. And bewildered with the grief-born dreams of the night, he cried out, "Woman, what hast thou done?"

Then, sweeter than the voice of doves among the fig-trees, came the voice of Esther: "Didst thou not bid me, husband, that I should choose and take away from thy house whatsoever I most desired? And I have chosen thee, and have brought thee hither, to my father's home, . . . loving thee more than all else in the world. Wilt thou drive me from thee now?" And he could not see her face for tears of love; yet he heard her voice speaking on, — speaking the golden words of Ruth, which are so old yet so young to the hearts of all that love : "*Whithersoever thou shalt go, I will also go; and whithersoever thou shalt dwell, I also will dwell.* And the Angel of Death only may part us; for thou art all in all to me.". . .

And in the golden sunlight at the doorway suddenly stood, like a statue of Babylonian silver, the grand gray figure of Rabbi Simon ben Yochai, lifting his hands in benediction.

"*Schmah Israel!* — the Lord our God, who is One, bless ye with everlasting benediction! May your hearts be welded by love, as gold with gold by the cunning of goldsmiths! May the Lord, who coupleth and setteth the single in families, watch over ye! The Lord make this valiant woman even as Rachel and as Lia, who built up the house of Israel! And ye shall behold your children and your children's children in the House of the Lord!"

Even so the Lord blessed them; and Esther became as the fruitful vine, and they saw their children's children in Israel. Forasmuch as it is written: "He will regard the prayer of the destitute."

14

THE DISPUTE IN THE HALACHA.

... Told of in the Book BAVA-METZIA; *or, "The Middle Gate"*
of the Holy Shas. . . . The Lord loveth the gates that are marked
with the Halacha more than the synagogues and the schools.

Now, in those days there was a dispute between the Mishnic Doctors and Rabbi Eliezer
concerning the legal cleanliness of a certain
bake-oven, as is written in the Bava-Metzia of
the Talmud. For while all the others held the
oven to be unclean according to the Halacha,
Rabbi Eliezer declared that it was clean ; and
all their arguments he overthrew, and all their
objections he confuted, although they would not
suffer themselves to be convinced. Then did
Rabbi Eliezer at last summon a carob-tree to
bear witness to his interpretation of the law ; and
the carob-tree uprooted itself, and rose in air with
the clay trickling from its roots, and moved
through air to the distance of four hundred yards,
and replanted itself, trembling, in the soil.

But the Doctors of the Mishna, being used to
marvellous things, were little moved ; and they
said : "We may not admit the testimony of a
carob-tree. Shall a carob-tree discourse to us

regarding the Halacha? Will a carob-tree teach
us the law?"

Then said Rabbi Eliezer to the brook that mut-
tered its unceasing prayer without: "Bear me
witness, O thou running water!" And the rivu-
let changed the course of its current; its waters
receded, and, flowing back to their fountain-head,
left naked the pebbles of their bed to dry under
the sun.

But the Disciples of the Sages still held to their
first opinion, saying: "Shall a brook prattle to
us of law? Shall we hearken to the voice of running water rather than to the voice of the Holy
One — blessed be He! — and of His servant
Moses?"

Then Rabbi Eliezer, lifting his eyes toward the
walls above, bearing holy words written upon
them, cried out: "Yet bear me witness also,
ye consecrated walls, that I have decided aright
in this matter!" And the walls quivered, bent
inward, curved like a bellying sail in the moment
of a changing wind, impended above the hands of
the Rabbis, and would have fallen had not Rabbi
Joshuah rebuked them, saying: "What is it to
you if the Rabbis do wrangle in the Halacha?
Would ye crush us? Be ye still!" So the walls,
obeying Rabbi Joshuah, would not fall; but

neither would they return to their former place, forasmuch as they obeyed Rabbi Eliezer also, — so that they remain toppling even unto this day.

Then, seeing that their hearts were hardened against him even more than the stones of the building, Rabbi Eliezer cried out: "*Let the Bath-Kol decide between us!*" Whereupon the college shook to its foundation; and a Voice from heaven answered, saying: "What have ye to do with Rabbi Eliezer? for in all things the Halacha is even according to his decision!"

But Rabbi Joshuah stood upon his feet fearlessly in the midst, and said: "It is not lawful that even a Voice from heaven should be regarded by us. For Thou, O God, didst long ago write down in the law which Thou gavest upon Sinai, saying, '*Thou shalt follow the multitude.*'" And they would not hearken unto Rabbi Eliezer; but they did excommunicate him, and did commit all his decisions regarding the law to be consumed with fire.

[Now some have it that Rabbi Nathan testified that the Prophet Elijah declared unto him that God Himself was deceived in this matter, and acknowledged error in His decision, saying: "My children have vanquished me! my children have prevailed against me!" But as we also know

that in punishment for the excommunication of
Rabbi Eliezer a third portion of all the barley
and of the olives and of the wheat in the whole
world was smitten with blight, we may well believe that Rabbi Eliezer was not in error.]

***

Now, while yet under sentence of excommunication, Rabbi Eliezer fell grievously ill; and the
Rabbonim knew nothing of it. Yet such was his
learning, that Rabbi Akiva and all the disciples
of the latter came unto him to seek instruction.
. . . Then Rabbi Eliezer, rising upon his elbow,
asked them, "Wherefore came ye hither?"

"We came that we might learn the Halacha,"
answered Akiva.

"But wherefore came ye not sooner?"

And they answered, "Because we had not
time."

Then Rabbi Eliezer, feeling wroth at the reply,
said to them also: "Verily, if ye die a natural
death, I shall marvel greatly. And as for thee,
Akiva, thy death shall be the worst of all! It is
well for thee that I do not give thee my malediction, seeing thou hast dared to say that one may
not have time to learn the law!"

And Rabbi Eliezer, folding his arms upon his
breast to die, continued: "Woe! woe is me!

woe unto these two arms of mine, that they are now even as two scrolls of the law rolled up, whereof the contents are hidden! Had ye waited upon me before, ye might have learned many strange things; and now my knowledge must perish with me! Much have I learned, and much have I taught, yet always without diminishing the knowledge of my Rabbis by even so much as the waters of the ocean might be diminished by the lapping of a dog!"...

And he continued to speak to them: "Now, over and above all those things, I did expound three thousand Halachoth in regard to the growing of Egyptian cucumbers; and yet none save only Rabbi Akiva ben Joseph ever asked me so much as one question regarding them!... We were walking on the road between the fields, when he asked me to instruct him regarding Egyptian cucumbers. Then I uttered but one word; and, behold! the fields forthwith became full of Egyptian cucumbers. He asked me concerning the gathering of them. I uttered but one word; and, lo! all the cucumbers did gather themselves into one place before me."...

And even as Rabbi Eliezer was thus speaking, his soul departed from him; and Rabbi Akiva with all his disciples mourned bitterly for him and for themselves, seeing they had indeed come too late to learn the law.

*_**

But the prediction of Rabbi Eliezer was fulfilled. . . . For it came to pass, when Rabbi Akiva had become a most holy man, and marvellously learned, that the Romans forbade the teaching of the law in Israel; and Rabbi Akiva persisted in teaching it publicly to the people, saying: "If we suffer so much by the will of the Holy One — blessed be He! — while studying the law, how much indeed shall we suffer while neglecting it!"

So they led him out to execution, and tortured him with tortures unspeakable. Now it was just at that hour when the prayer must be said: *"Hear, O Israel! the Lord our God is One."*

And even while they were tearing his flesh with combs of iron, Rabbi Akiva uttered the holy words and died. And there came a mighty Voice from heaven, crying: "Blessed art thou, O Rabbi Akiva, for thy soul and the word ONE left thy body together!"

RABBI YOCHANAN BEN ZACHAI.

*There is in Heaven a certain living creature which hath letters
upon its forehead. And by day these letters, which are brighter
than the sun, form the word TRUTH, whereby the angels know
that it is day. But when evening cometh, the letters, self-changing,
do shape themselves into the word FAITH, whereby the angels
know that the night cometh. . . .*

Now Hillel the Great, who gathered together
the Sedarim of the Talmud, and who was also the
teacher of that Jesus the Gentiles worship, had
eighty other disciples who became holy men. Of
these, thirty were indeed so holy that the Shechinah rested upon them even as upon Moses, so
that their faces gave out light; and rays like
beams of the sun streamed from their temples.

And of thirty others it is said their holiness was
as the holiness of Joshua, the son of Nun, being
worthy that the sun should stand still at their
behest. And the remaining twenty, of whom the
greatest was Rabbi Jonathan ben Uzziel, and the
least of all Rabbi Yochanan ben Zachai, were
held to be only of middling worth. Yet there is
now not one worthy to compare with the least of
them, seeing that Rabbi Yochanan was holier
than living man to-day.

For, humble as he was, Rabbi Yochanan ben
Zachai was deeply learned in the Scriptures, — in
the Mishna and the Gemara and the Midrashim,
— in the Kabbalah, the rules of Gematria, of
Notricon, and of Temurah, — in the five mystic
alphabets, Atbash, Atbach, Albam, Aiakbechar,
Tashrak, — in legends and the lesser laws and
the niceties, — in the theories of the moon, in the
language of angels and the whispering of palm-
trees and the speech of demons. And if all the
seas were ink, and all the reeds that shake by
rivers were pens, and all the men of the earth
were scribes, never could they write down all that
Rabbi Yochanan ben Zachai had learned, nor
even so much of it as he taught in his lifetime,
which endured for the period of one hundred and
twenty years. Yet he was the least of all the
disciples of Hillel.

Of the years of his life the first forty he devoted
to worldly things, especially to commerce, that he
might earn enough to enable him to devote unto
good works the remainder of the time allotted
him. And the next forty years he devoted to
study, becoming so learned that he was indeed
accused of being a magician, as were also those
Rabbis who, by combination of the letters of the
Name Ineffable, did create living animals and

fruits, — as were also Rav Oshayah and Rav Chaneanah, who by study of the Book Yetzirah (which is the Book of Creation) did create for themselves a calf, and did eat thereof.

And the last forty years of his most holy life Rabbi Yochanan gave to teaching the people.

***

Now, as it is related in the Book Bava Bathra, in Seder Nezikin of the Talmud, Rabbi Yochanan ben Zachai did upon one occasion explain before a vain disciple the words of the Prophet Isaiah. And so explaining he said: "The Most Holy — blessed be His name forever! — shall take precious stones and pearls, each measuring thirty cubits by thirty cubits, and shall cut and polish them till they measure twenty cubits by ten cubits each, and shall set them in the gates of Jerusalem."

Then the vain and foolish disciple, the son of Impudence, laughed loudly, and with mockery in his voice said: "What man hath ever seen an emerald or a diamond, a ruby or a pearl, even so large as the egg of a small bird? and wilt thou indeed tell us that there be jewels thirty cubits by thirty?" But Rabbi Yochanan returned no answer; and the disciple, mocking, departed.

Now, some days after these things happened, that wicked disciple went upon a voyage; for he was in commerce and a great driver of bargains, and known in many countries for his skill in bartering and his ability in finding objects of price. Now, while in his vessel, when the sailors slumbered, waiting to raise the anchor at dawn, it was given to that wicked disciple to see a great light below the waters. And looking down he saw mighty angels in the depths of the sea, quarrying monstrous diamonds and emeralds, and opening prodigious shells to obtain enormous pearls. And the eyes of the angels were fixed upon him, even as they worked below the water in that awful light. Then a dreadful fear came upon him, so that his knees smote one against another, and his teeth fell out ; and in obedience to a power that moved his tongue against his will, he cried aloud : " For what are those diamonds and those mighty emeralds? For what are those monstrous pearls?" And a Voice answered him from the deep, " For the gates of Jerusalem!"

And having returned from his voyage, the disciple hastened with all speed to the place where Rabbi Yochanan ben Zachai was teaching, and told him that which he had seen, and vowed that the words of Rabbi Yochanan should nevermore be doubted by him.

But the Rabbi, seeing into his heart, and beholding the blackness of the wickedness within it, answered in a voice of thunder: " Raca! hadst thou not seen them, thou wouldst even now mock the words of the sages!" And with a single glance of his eye he consumed that wicked disciple as a dry leaf is consumed by flame, reducing the carcass of his body to a heap of smoking ashes as though it had been smitten by the lightning of the Lord.

And the people marvelled exceedingly. But Rabbi Yochanan ben Zachai, paying no heed to the white ashes smoking at his feet, continued to explain unto his disciples the language of palm-trees and of demons.

A TRADITION OF TITUS.

. . . Which is in the Book GITTIN *of the Talmud. . . . Before Titus the world was like unto the eyeball of man; the ocean being as the white, the world as the black, the pupil thereof Jerusalem, and the image within the pupil the Temple of the Lord. . . .*

VERILY hath it been said, in Chullin of the Holy Shas, that "sixty iron mines are suspended in the sting of a gnat."

For in those days Titus — may his ears be made
into sockets for the hinges of Gehenna to turn
upon! — came from Rome with his idolaters, and
laid siege to the Holy City, and destroyed it, and
bore away the virgins into captivity. He who
had not beheld Jerusalem before that day had not
seen the glory of Israel.

There were three hundred and ninety-four synagogues, and three hundred and ninety-four courts
of law, and the same number of academies for the
youth. . . . When the gates of the temple were
opened, the roar of their golden hinges was heard
at the distance of eight Sabbath days' journey. . . .
The Veil of the Holy of Holies was woven by
eighty-two myriads of virgins; three hundred
priests were needed to draw it, and three hundred to lave it when soiled. But Titus — be his
name accursed forever! — wrapped up the sacred
vessels in it, and, putting them in a ship, set sail
for the city of Rome. . . .

Scarcely had he departed beyond sight of the
land when a great storm arose, — the deeps made
visible their darkness, the waves showed their
teeth! And an exceeding great fear came upon
the mariners, and they cried out, "It is the
Elohim!"

But Titus, mocking, lifted his voice against

Heaven, and the thunders, and the lightnings, and the mutterings of the sea, exclaiming: " Lo! this God of Jews hath no power save on water! Pharaoh He drowned; Sisera He drowned also; even now He seeketh to drown me with my legions! If He be mighty, and not afraid to strive with me on land, let Him rather await me on solid earth, and there see whether He be strong enough to prevail against me." (Now Sisera, indeed, was not drowned; but Titus, being ignorant and an idolater, spake falsely.)

Then burst forth a splendor of white fire from the darkness of the clouds; and deeper than the thunder a Voice answered unto him: "O thou wicked one, son of a wicked man and grandson of Esau the wicked, go thou ashore! Lo! I have a creature awaiting thee, which is but little and insignificant in my world; go thou and fight with it!"

And the tempest ceased.

So Titus and his legions landed after many days upon the shore of the land called Italy,—the shore that vibrated forever to the sound of the mighty city of Rome, whereof the Voice was heard unto the four ends of the earth, and the din whereof deafened Rabbi Yehoshuah even at the distance of a hundred and twenty miles. For in

Rome there were three hundred and sixty-five streets, and in each street three hundred and sixty-five palaces, and leading up to the pillared portico of each palace a marble flight of three hundred and sixty-five steps.

But no sooner had the Emperor Titus placed his foot upon the shore than there attacked him a gnat! And the gnat flew up his nostrils, and entered into his wicked brain, and gnawed it, and tortured him with unspeakable torture. And he could obtain no cessation of his anguish; neither was there any physician in Rome who could do aught to relieve him. So the gnat abode in his brain for seven years, and the face of Titus became, for everlasting pain, as the face of a man in hell.

⁎

Now, after Titus had vainly sacrificed unto all the obscene gods of the Romans, it came to pass that he heard one day, within a blacksmith's shop, the sound of the hammer descending upon the anvil; and the sound was grateful to his ears as the harping of David unto the hearing of Saul, and the anguish presently departed from him. Then, thinking unto himself, he exclaimed, "Lo! I have found relief;" and having offered sacrifices unto the Smith-god, he ordered the smith to be brought to his palace, together with anvils

and hammers. And he paid the smith four zou-
zim a day — as money is reckoned in Israel — to
hammer for him.

But the smith could not hammer unceasingly;
and whenever he stopped the pain returned, and
the gnat tormented exceedingly. So other smiths
were sent for; and at last a Jewish smith. who
was a slave. To him Titus would pay nothing,
notwithstanding he had paid the Gentiles; for he
said, "It is enough payment for thee to behold
thy enemy suffer!"

Yet thirty days more; and no sound of hammers could lessen the agony of the gnawing of
the gnat, and Titus knew that he must die.

Then he bade his family that they should burn
his body after he was dead, and collect the ashes,
and send out seven ships to scatter the ashes
upon the waves of the Seven Seas, lest the God
of Israel should resurrect his body at the Day of
Judgment.

***

[But it is written in Midrash Kohelet, of the
holy Midrashim, that Hadrian — may his name
be blotted out! — once asked Rabbi Joshua ben
Chanania, "From what shall the body be reconstructed at the Last Day?" And the Rabbi answered, "From Luz in the backbone." When

Hadrian demanded proof, the Rabbi took Luz, the little bone of the spine, and immersed it in water, and it was not softened. He put it into the fire, and it was not consumed. He put it into a mill, and it could not be ground. He hammered it upon an anvil; but the hammer was broken, and the anvil split asunder.

Therefore the desire of Titus shall not prevail; and the Lord will surely reconstruct his body for punishment out of Luz in the backbone!]

* *

But before they burned the corpse of Titus they opened his skull and looked into his brain, that they might find the gnat.

Now the gnat was as big as a swallow, and weighed two *selas*, as weight is reckoned in Israel. And they found that its claws were of brass, and the jaws of its mouth were of iron!

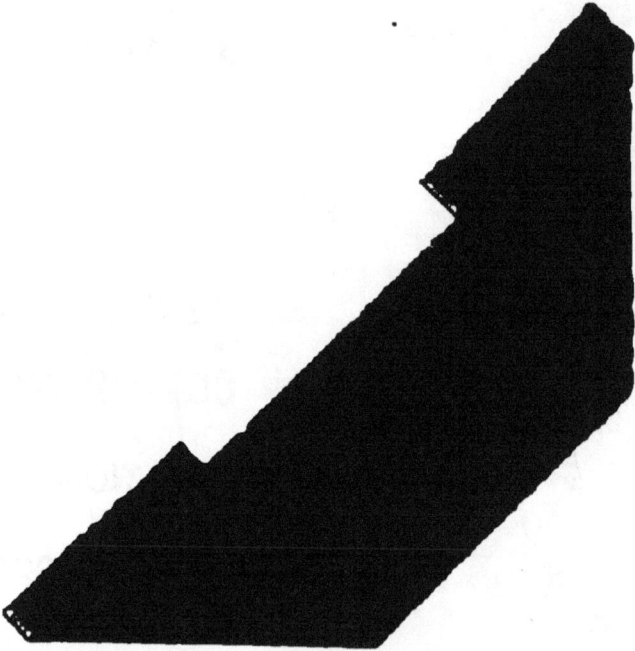

www.ingramcontent.com/pod-product-compliance
Lightning Source LLC
Chambersburg PA
CBHW030319270326
41926CB00010B/1425